Supervising the Trainee Appraiser:

National Regulations and Responsibilities

HONDROS LEARNING™

4140 Executive Parkway

Westerville, Ohio 43081

www.hondroslearning.com

18 17 16   2 3 4

ISBN: 978-1-59844-244-1

For more information on or to purchase our products, please visit www.hondroslearning.com.

TABLE OF CONTENTS

Supervising the Trainee Appraiser: National Regulations and Responsibilities addresses the national topic areas for supervisory appraisers and trainee appraisers specified by the Appraiser Qualifications Board (AQB) of The Appraisal Foundation in the *2015 Real Property Appraiser Qualifications Criteria*. Other coursework discussing the similarities and differences of specific jurisdictional qualifying regulations may supplement this course.

The course commences with an overview of national and state appraisal regulatory bodies as well as a comprehensive discussion of the minimum AQB qualifying criteria for supervisory appraisers and the various appraiser classifications. Obligations of appraiser ethics and competency are also discussed with a focus on supervisory appraisers and trainees. The course concludes with specific roles and responsibilities of supervisory appraisers and trainee appraisers, including a final chapter that serves as a best practices checklist, designed to ensure thorough and meaningful supervisory oversight, and best practice development by trainees in appraisal development and reporting.

Hondros Learning

Hondros Learning™ is a leading provider of classroom materials for appraisal pre-licensing and continuing education. Together with Hondros College of Business, we have provided training and educational products for more than one million students. For more information about CompuCram test preparation products or any of our other products, please visit www.hondroslearning.com, www.compucram.com.

Course Learning Objectives

- Define the regulatory structure of appraiser licensing and certification.
- Describe the AQB's minimum qualifying criteria for appraisers.
- Identify the organizations and their roles in regulating the appraisal process.
- Identify specific qualifying requirements for supervisory appraisers and trainee appraisers.
- Specify the obligations of the ETHICS RULE and RECORD KEEPING RULE of USPAP and how they relate to supervisory appraisers and trainee appraisers.
- Describe the obligations of the COMPETENCY RULE and the SCOPE OF WORK RULE and how they relate to supervisory appraisers and trainee appraisers.
- Describe certain Standards Rules of USPAP and how they relate to supervisory appraisers and trainee appraisers.
- Define Advisory Opinion 31 and how it relates to supervisory appraisers and trainee appraisers.
- Describe the ethical obligations of supervisory appraisers and trainee appraisers as presented in the ETHICS RULE.
- Identify the responsibilities of supervisory appraisers and trainees revealed in fair housing and fair lending practices.
- Define the specific responsibilities of supervisory appraisers.
- Identify the specific duties and responsibilities of trainee appraisers.
- Describe the assignment responsibilities required in general development and reporting.
- Identify valuation analysis and reporting responsibilities.

Exam Prep

Additional appraisal products available from Hondros Learning to help students prepare for the licensing exam include the *Appraisal Review Crammer*™, *4th edition*—a valuable self-study or classroom exam preparation guide; and *CompuCram*™ *Appraisal Exam Prep Software.*

Acknowledgments

Hondros Learning™ thanks the following expert for his valuable contributions and assistance in developing this text:

Timothy Detty

Lead Appraisal Instructor, Hondros College

Tim Detty has taught thousands of real estate and appraisal students over the course of his teaching career at Hondros College. A practicing Certified General Appraiser, he has also written numerous real estate and ap-praisal courses and served as both author and expert reviewer for several real estate and appraisal textbooks. He has been awarded the designation of Certified Distance Education Instructor (CDEI) from the International Dis-tance Education Certification Center (IDECC) and is a member of the National Association of Appraisers. In addition to being an AQB Certified USPAP Instructor, Tim is a frequent guest lecturer and contributor to vari-ous real estate and appraisal publications.

Chapter 1

Qualifications and Obligations

Appraiser qualifications to obtain and keep a license or certification are derived from a combination of two sources: **National authority** and **state authority**. From the national perspective, The Appraisal Foundation establishes the basic qualifying standards, while the state level adopts these standards and **often adds additional qualifying standards**.

Supervisory appraiser and trainee appraiser candidates must also be familiar with specific requirements of their respective jurisdictions regarding qualifications and other differing regulations. **The Appraisal Subcommittee**, created as a result of **FIRREA**, *oversees state appraisal regulatory agencies with the charge to ensure states are in compliance with the qualifications standards promulgated by The Appraisal Foundation.*

This chapter will provide an overview of the Appraisal Qualifications Board's minimum credential requirements for appraisers.

Chapter Objectives

After completing this chapter, you will be able to:

- Define the regulatory structure of appraiser licensing and certification.
- Describe the AQB's minimum qualifying criteria for appraisers.
- Identify the organizations and their roles in regulating the appraisal process.

Key Terms

The Appraisal Foundation (TAF) A nonprofit private organization which is recognized by Congress as the authority for professional appraisal standards and appraiser qualifications.

Appraisal Practices Board An independent board of The Appraisal Foundation which is responsible for identifying and issuing opinions on Recognized Valuation Methods and Techniques, which may apply to all disciplines within the appraisal profession.

Appraiser Qualifications Board (AQB) An independent board of The Appraisal Foundation which is responsible for establishing minimum education, experience, and other criteria for certification and recertification of qualified appraisers.

Appraisal Standards Board (ASB) An independent board of The Appraisal Foundation which is responsible for the subject, style, content, and substance of USPAP and other communications related to appraisal standards, including Advisory Opinions and FAQs.

Appraisal Subcommittee Created as a result of the Financial Institutions Reform, Recovery, and Enforcement Act (FIRREA) to provide federal oversight of state appraiser regulatory programs and a monitoring framework for the Appraisal Foundation and the Federal Financial Institutions Regulatory Agencies in their roles to protect federal financial and public policy interests in real estate appraisals utilized in federally related transactions.

(Continued on page 3)

The Appraisal Foundation

Prior to the creation of **The Appraisal Foundation (TAF)**, *a nonprofit private organization that is recognized by Congress as the authority for professional appraisal standards and appraiser qualifications*, and of the **Uniform Standards of Professional Appraisal Practice (USPAP)**, professional appraisal organizations which had standards of practice for their members, recognized the need for a **common set of standards**, as well as a **mechanism to enforce those standards**.

Eight U.S.-based appraisal organizations and the Appraisal Institute of Canada formed an ad hoc committee to develop what would, in 1987, become **USPAP**, *the professional appraisal standards promulgated by The Appraisal Foundation, and widely recognized throughout the United States as accepted standards of appraisal practice.*

This group further recognized:

- A new organization would be needed to achieve public recognition.
- The new organization would have independent authority over the standards and place the public's benefit ahead of any other interest.

The Appraisal Foundation Boards

This new organization was named The Appraisal Foundation, which at its time of creation had three boards:

1. Board of Trustees (BOT)
2. Appraiser Qualifications Board (AQB)
3. Appraisal Standards Board (ASB)

A fourth board was more recently added:

4. Appraisal Practices Board (APB)

Board of Trustees

The **Board of Trustees (BOT)** is *the governing body of The Appraisal Foundation*. The BOT:

1. Appoints members to the APB, AQB, and the ASB.
2. Ensures financing of TAF.
3. Monitors performance and oversight of TAF and its boards and advisory councils.

Appraiser Qualifications Board

The **Appraiser Qualifications Board (AQB)**:

- Establishes minimum education, experience, and other criteria for certification and recertification of qualified appraisers.
- Defines, issues, and promotes such qualification criteria.
- Disseminates such qualification criteria to states, government entities, and others.
- Creates and maintains the National Uniform Licensing and Certification Appraisal Examination.
- Maintains responsibility for the administration of the 7- and 15-hour National USPAP Courses and the Instructor Certification Program.
- Certifies National USPAP instructors.
- Administers the National Course Approval Program (CAP).
- Administers the National Undergraduate/Graduate Degree in Real Estate Program.
- Writes semi-annual Q&As in response to questions received regarding the *Real Property Appraiser Qualification Criteria*, National Uniform Licensing and Certification Examinations, CAP, or any other AQB-related issue or program.

As was mentioned, The AQB publishes periodic Q&As, which can be found on The Appraisal Foundation's website, located at http://www.appraisalfoundation.org

Throughout this course, several of the Q&As from that publication have been reproduced for study, as they are extremely valuable in understanding the qualifications, especially as they apply to supervisory appraisers and trainee appraisers and provide reinforcement that jurisdictional requirements may be greater or stricter.

√ **Note:** The AQB Q&As have been numbered for the purposes of this course.

Appraisal Standards Board

The **Appraisal Standards Board (ASB):**

- Establishes, improves, and promulgates USPAP.

- Is responsible for the subject, style, content, and substance of USPAP and other communications related to appraisal standards, including Advisory Opinions and FAQs.

- Writes periodic Q&As in response to questions received regarding USPAP.

- Issues exposure drafts for public comment of proposed changes to USPAP.

Obviously, compliance with USPAP is fundamental to a satisfactory appraiser trainee experience. Likewise, supervisory appraisers have an obligation to ensure their practices are in compliance, as well as that of the trainee.

Appraisal Practices Board

The **Appraisal Practices Board (APB):**

- Is responsible for identifying and issuing opinions on Recognized Valuation Methods and Techniques, which may apply to all disciplines within the appraisal profession.

- Offers voluntary guidance in topic areas that appraisers and users of appraisal services consider most significant.

- Utilizes panels of Subject Matter Experts (SMEs), who are widely recognized individuals with expertise in the specific topic being considered.

- Evaluates various issues through a public exposure process and ultimately adopts guidance that may include more than one recognized method or technique that addresses the specific topic.

Financial Institutions Reform, Recovery and Enforcement Act (FIRREA) An act passed in 1989 as a comprehensive savings and loan bailout and preventive measure against future S&L insolvency. This act recognizes USPAP as the industry standard for appraisals, and identifies the Appraisal Foundation as the authority for professional appraisal standards.

Guide Notes Guidance or advice provided by the AQB for assistance in understanding and implementing the Criteria. *

Real Property Appraiser Qualification Criteria (Criteria) Established by the Appraiser Qualifications Board (AQB) of The Appraisal Foundation, these Criteria set forth the minimum education, experience and examination requirements for real property appraisers. *

Required Core Curriculum A set of appraisal subject matter major headings known as "modules" which require a specified number of educational hours at each credential level. *

Uniform Standards of Professional Appraisal Practice (USPAP) Professional appraisal standards promulgated by The Appraisal Foundation, and widely recognized throughout the United States as accepted standards of appraisal practice.

* 2015 Real Property Appraiser Qualification Criteria – Appraiser Qualifications Board

Key Terms

The development standards of USPAP require the application of recognized methods and techniques in appraisal practice. The APB offers guidance to assist appraisers, including supervisory appraisers and trainee appraisers, to recognize methods and techniques which have been generally accepted by the APB.

√ **Note:** Valuation Advisories issued to date by the APB may also be found at http://www.appraisalfoundation.org

Other Appraisal Regulatory Bodies

In addition to the AQB, two other bodies outside of The Appraisal Foundation are integral to appraiser qualifications:

- Appraisal Subcommittee (ASC)
- State Appraiser Regulatory Agencies

The **Appraisal Subcommittee (ASC)** was created as a result of the Financial Institutions Reform, Recovery, and Enforcement Act (FIRREA).

Roles of the ASC include:
- Maintaining the official national registry of state licensed and certified real property appraisers.
- Overseeing the activities of state real estate appraiser licensing and certification agencies.

While the Appraiser Qualifications Board (AQB) and the Appraisal Standards Board (ASB) have all authority over appraiser qualifications and appraisal standards, state regulatory agencies can develop and impose greater criteria, and often do.

State regulatory agencies:

- Validate qualifications.
- Issue credentials.
- Investigate complaints.
- Take disciplinary action.
- Impose and enforce USPAP.

Again, it is important to remember that individual jurisdictions may have differing, greater qualifications and performance standards than those established by the ASB and the AQB.

AQB Appraiser Classifications & Qualifications

There are four permitted appraiser classifications addressed by the AQB:

- Trainee Appraiser
- Licensed Residential Real Property Appraiser
- Certified Residential Real Property Appraiser
- Certified General Real Property Appraiser

√ **Note:** Some states may not offer all of the classifications noted, or may refer to them in a slightly different manner.

The AQB of The Appraisal Foundation has certain minimum requirements that must be met in order to obtain a license or certification, including a trainee credential. Each state must meet, *at a minimum*, the requirements of the AQB. All states then have the option to implement greater standards beyond what is required by the AQB.

The AQB sets **minimum standards** for appraisers, which include four major components:

1. Qualifying education
2. Experience
3. Continuing education
4. Examination

> √ **Note:** The minimum standards are communicated through the Real Property Appraiser Qualification Criteria are discussed in this chapter and available at The Appraisal Foundation's website.

The AQB enhanced the requirements for qualifying education hours, qualifying education curriculum, and college course requirements for licensed and certified appraisers. The new requirements were effective beginning January 1, 2008, although some states implemented them prior to that date.

In its December 2011 meeting, the AQB revised the 2008 requirements. Although there were various modifications to the criteria, the most noticeable was the inclusion of college education hours or a college degree required for qualification as an appraiser.

- For the **Licensed Residential** level, an *Associate's degree or 30 college semester hours* are required.
- For the **Certified** levels, a *Bachelor's degree* is required.

The changes are effective at the national level on **January 1, 2015**

2015 Real Property Appraiser Qualification Criteria

The 2015 **Real Property Appraiser Qualification Criteria** (Criteria) is a *comprehensive compilation of appraiser qualification criteria and references pre-license and post-license obligations for appraisers.*

In general, the criteria are categorized as:

- Criteria Applicable to All Real Property Appraiser Classifications (including continuing education).
- Education, Experience, and Examination Requirements for All Appraiser Classifications.
- Supervisory Appraiser and Trainee Appraiser Requirements.

Criteria Applicable to All Real Property Appraiser Classifications

Appraisers must perform and practice in compliance with USPAP. Existing credential holders (with the exception of trainee appraisers) in good standing in any jurisdiction shall be considered in compliance with current AQB criteria *if they have passed an AQB-approved qualifying examination for that credential.* With the **exception of trainee appraisers**, this applies to reciprocity, temporary practice, renewals, and applications for the same credential in another jurisdiction.

> √ **Caution!** All credential holders must comply with ongoing requirements for continuing education and state renewal procedures.

Qualifying and continuing education may be obtained only from:

- Colleges or universities
- Community or junior colleges
- Real estate appraisal or real estate related organizations
- State or federal agencies or commissions
- Proprietary schools
- Providers approved by state certification/ licensing agencies
- The Appraisal Foundation or its Boards

√ **Note:** Experience may **not** be substituted for education. Education may be from classroom or distance education acceptable to the 2015 Criteria.

Criteria Specific to Qualifying Education

The following are highlights of the criteria:

- Class hours will be credited only for education courses with content that follows the **Required Core Curriculum** for each respective credential classification.

- Credit toward qualifying education requirements may also be obtained via the completion of a degree in Real Estate from an accredited degree-granting college or university approved by the Association to Advance Collegiate Schools of Business, or a regional or national accreditation agency recognized by the U.S. Secretary of Education, **provided that the college or university has had its curriculum reviewed and approved by the AQB.**

Class hours may be obtained only where the minimum length of the course is at least **15 hours**, and the individual successfully completes a proctored, closed-book final examination for the course.

√ **Note:** Courses taken to satisfy the qualifying education requirements must **not** be repetitive.

Applicants must take the *15-Hour National USPAP Course*, or its AQB-approved equivalent, and pass the associated *15-Hour National USPAP Course* examination.

Distance education courses for use as qualifying education must include a **written, closed-book final examination** (proctored by an official approved by the college or university, or by the sponsoring organization), in compliance with the AQB's examination requirements.

Guide notes are *provided by the AQB to assist in understanding and implementing qualification criteria.* **Guide Note 1** of the Real Property Appraiser Qualification Criteria offers a comprehensive overview of required core course content on page 71. This guidebook can be downloaded by visiting www.appraisalfoundation.org and searching for "Real Property Appraisers Qualification Criteria."

Common questions and answers posted by the AQB will follow. As noted earlier in the chapter, these Q&As are included to further alleviate confusion, and round out the comprehension of the criteria and chapter content.

AQB Q&A #1

I am a Trainee Appraiser preparing to get my Certified Residential credential. For my initial qualifying education to become a Trainee Appraiser, I completed 80 hours of *Basic Appraisal Principles and Procedures* in 2003 from a proprietary school that no longer exists. My state appraiser regulatory agency said any courses taken before the current edition of the *Real Property Appraiser Qualification Criteria* were no longer considered valid according to the AQB. Why can't these original hours count toward the qualifying education requirement for my Certified Residential credential?

Response:

The *Criteria* do not contain any provision that invalidates qualifying education successfully completed prior to the effective date of the *Criteria* for existing credential holders. As with all AQB *Criteria*, states may create requirements that are more restrictive; if so, you'll need to clarify this with your state. From the AQB's perspective, in this case, courses that were eligible in 2003 would remain valid towards the current *Criteria*.

However, the *Criteria* do include the following provision affecting non-credentialed appraisers: "All qualifying education must be completed within the **five (5) year period** prior to the date of submission of a trainee appraiser application." In this case, an appraiser pursuing a trainee appraiser credential would **not** be able to use courses more than **5 years old** at the time of submission of the application to become a trainee appraiser.

AQB Q&A #2

I have an appraisal credential in my home state and I am now seeking to obtain a credential in a new state where I will be relocating. My appraisal coursework was approved in my home state, but I am having difficulty getting my qualifying education approved in my new state. If one state approved my courses doesn't that mean they are automatically accepted by other states?

Response:

The *Real Property Appraiser Qualification Criteria* states "Existing credential holders (with the exception of Trainee appraisers) in good standing in any jurisdiction shall be considered in compliance with current *Real Property Appraiser Qualification Criteria (Criteria)* if they have passed an AQB-approved qualifying examination for that credential. This applies to reciprocity, temporary practice, renewals, and applications for the same credential (with the exception of Trainee appraisers) in another jurisdiction."

However, while the above represents the position of the Appraiser Qualifications Board, each state has the right to regulate commerce within its boundaries. Thus, their laws may require an applicant to "start from scratch" and fulfill all of the current requirements for licensure or certification.

Furthermore, each state has the responsibility to approve qualifying education courses leading toward real property appraiser credentials. Individual course providers (e.g. colleges/universities, proprietary schools, designation organizations) must seek approval of their courses by individual states. As such, it is possible one state may have approved a course, while another has not.

Continuing Education Criteria

There are numerous points in the 2015 qualification criteria specific to continuing education. The following are highlights of the criteria:

- Aside from complying with the requirements to complete the *7-Hour National USPAP Update Course*, or its equivalent, appraisers may **not** receive credit for completion of *the same continuing education course offering within an appraiser's continuing education cycle*.

Credit towards continuing education hour requirements for each appraiser classification may be granted only where the length of the educational offering is at least **two (2) hours**.

Acceptable continuing education topics include, but are not limited to:

- Ad valorem taxation
- Arbitration, dispute resolution
- Courses related to the practice of real estate appraisal or consulting
- Development cost estimating
- Ethics and standards of professional practice - USPAP
- Land use planning, zoning
- Management, leasing, timesharing
- Property development, partial interests
- Real estate law, easements, and legal interests
- Real estate litigation, damages, condemnation
- Real estate financing and investment
- Real estate appraisal-related computer applications
- Real estate securities and syndication
- Developing opinions of real property value in appraisals that also include personal property and/or business value
- Seller concessions and impact on value
- Energy efficient items and "green building" appraisals

Educational offerings taken for upgrading a current classification may be simultaneously counted towards the continuing education requirement for a current classification.

For continuing education courses taken via distance education, at least a written examination proctored by an acceptable individual must be taken (oral exams are not acceptable) **or** successful completion of prescribed course mechanisms required to demonstrate knowledge of the subject matter must be integral to the course.

Appraisers must successfully complete the *7-Hour National USPAP Update Course*, or its AQB-approved equivalent, **every two calendar years**. Individuals who are credentialed in more than one jurisdiction shall **not** have to take more than one *7-Hour National USPAP Update Course* within a two-calendar year period for the purposes of meeting AQB *Criteria*.

The equivalent of **fourteen (14) class hours of instruction** in courses or seminars for each year during the period preceding the renewal is required. For example, a two-year continuing education cycle would require twenty-eight hours. The class hour requirement can be fulfilled at any time during the cycle.

Inactive Status

State appraiser regulatory agencies may place a credential holder in an "**inactive status**" in the event the state determines a deficiency in continuing education was due to extenuating circumstances. Prior to reactivation, credential holders in an inactive status *must complete all required continuing education hours that would have been required if the credential holder was in an active status*. The required hours must also include the most recent edition of a *7-Hour National USPAP Update Course* (or its AQB-approved equivalent).

Military Duty and Disaster Statuses

Waivers may **not** be granted to credential holders who have failed to meet the continuing education requirements.

Deferrals may **not** be granted to credential holders, except in the case of individuals returning from active military duty, or individuals impacted by a state- or federally-declared disaster.

State appraiser regulatory agencies may allow credential holders returning from active military duty to be placed in active status for a period of **up to 90 days** pending completion of all continuing education requirements. State appraiser regulatory agencies may allow credential holders impacted by a state- or federally-declared disaster that occurs within 90 days prior to the end of the continuing education cycle to remain (or be placed in) active status for a period of **up to 90 days** after the end of the credential holder's continuing education cycle, pending completion of all continuing education requirements.

Partial Year in a Continuing Education Cycle

Credentialed appraisers are required to complete continuing education for a partial year in a continuing education cycle as follows:

- For continuing education cycle periods of **185 days or more, 14 hours of continuing education** is required.

- For continuing education cycle periods of **less than 185 days, no hours of continuing education** are required.

Example #1:
A credential issued on August 15 that expires on December 31 of the same year **would not require any continuing education hours for that year**.

Example #2:
A credential issued on May 15 that expires on December 31 of the same year **would require 14 continuing education hours for that year**.

Example #3:

A credential issued on August 15 that expires on December 31 of the following year **would require 14 hours of continuing education to renew**.

State appraiser regulatory agencies may award continuing education credit to credentialed appraisers who attend a state appraiser regulatory agency meeting, under the following conditions:

- Credit may be awarded for a single state appraiser regulatory agency meeting per continuing education cycle.
- The meeting must be open to the public and must be a **minimum of two (2) hours** in length.
- The total credit **cannot exceed seven (7) hours** and the state appraiser regulatory agency must ensure that the credentialed appraiser attends the meeting for the required period of time.

AQB Q&A #3

I am a certified appraiser in a state with a 2-year licensure cycle. As such, I am required to complete 28 hours of approved continuing education (CE) in order to be eligible to renew my certification. If I complete more than the required 28 hours, can I carryover the extra hours to my next certification renewal?

Response:

No. The *Real Property Appraiser Qualification Criteria* does not provide for any carryover of CE hours from one renewal period to the next. Specifically, it states under *Section F. Criteria Specific to Continuing Education, Item 11* the instruction for which CE is sought to take place must do so "… during the period preceding the renewal…."

AQB Q&A #4

The *Real Property Appraiser Qualification Criteria* require that I take the *7-Hour National USPAP Update Course* every two calendar years. If I do not take the course until 18 months after the new version of USPAP goes into effect, does that mean I can continue to follow the prior version of USPAP until I take the update course?

Response:

No. You are responsible to comply with the version of USPAP from the date it becomes effective, regardless of when you complete the *7-Hour National USPAP Update Course.* For this reason, the AQB encourages all credential holders to complete the course as soon as possible, to ensure proper understanding of any revisions made to USPAP.

AQB Q&A #5

I am a state-certified appraiser and was told by my state appraiser regulatory agency the *15-Hour National USPAP Course* would not satisfy my continuing education requirement to complete the *7-Hour National USPAP Update Course*. Why can't I take the 15-Hour course in lieu of the 7-Hour course?

Response:

The *Real Property Appraiser Qualification Criteria* require the *7-Hour National USPAP Update Course* be taken for continuing education (CE) every two calendar years. The *7-Hour National USPAP Update Course* concentrates on the most recent changes to USPAP, common problem areas, and application of USPAP to real world situations. This course is appropriate for practicing appraisers who already have a baseline understanding of USPAP, but need to be apprised of recent developments and updates affecting their appraisal practice. The *15-Hour National USPAP Course* is geared to the beginning appraiser who has a limited understanding of USPAP. The coverage and treatment of changes or emerging issues is not the focus of this course; thus it does not meet the educational objectives of the 7-Hour course.

Generic Examination Criteria

A new applicant not currently licensed or certified and in good standing in another jurisdiction, shall have **up to 24 months**, after approval by the state, to take and pass an AQB-approved qualifying examination for the credential.

Successful completion of the examination is valid for a period of **24 months**.

Generic Experience Criteria

Education may **not** be substituted for experience, except for work without a traditional client (discussed later). The quantitative experience requirements must be satisfied by time spent on the appraisal process.

The appraisal process consists of:

* Analyzing factors that affect value.
* Defining the problem.
* Gathering and analyzing data.
* Applying the appropriate analysis and methodology.
* Arriving at an opinion and correctly reporting the opinion in compliance with USPAP.

Hours may be treated as cumulative in order to achieve the necessary number of hours of appraisal experience. Cumulative is defined as meaning that experience may be acquired over any time period.

The following is an example of cumulative experience:

Year 1:   200 Hours
Year 2:   800 Hours
Year 3:   600 Hours
Year 4:   400 Hours
Year 5:   500 Hours

Total: 2,500 Hours

There need not be a client in a traditional sense (i.e., a client hiring an appraiser for a business purpose) for an appraisal to qualify for experience, but experience gained for work without a traditional client cannot exceed **50%** of the total experience requirement. Practicum courses that are approved by the AQB Course Approval Program or state appraiser regulatory agencies can satisfy the non-traditional client experience requirement.

Experience credit shall be granted for the actual classroom hours of instruction, and hours of documented research and analysis as awarded from the practicum course approval process. An **hour of experience** is defined as *verifiable time spent in performing tasks in accordance with acceptable appraisal practice.*

Acceptable real property appraisal practice for experience credit includes:

* Appraisal
* Appraisal review
* Appraisal consulting
* Mass appraisal

All experience must be obtained after January 30, 1989, and must be USPAP-compliant.

AQB Q&A #6

I am employed by a county appraisal district where we value properties for ad valorem tax purposes. My job requirements include valuing real property using the sales comparison approach, performing on-site inspections of properties, using mass appraisal tools to assign real property values, analyzing sales on an annual basis, etc. Our state requires appraisal experience for state licensure or certification to comply with the Appraiser Qualifications Board (AQB) *Criteria* for acceptable experience. Does my position as a Residential Appraiser at the appraisal district meet the AQB *Criteria* for acceptable experience?

Response:

Just by serving in a municipal appraisal position, you are not automatically granted credit. Per the *Real Property Appraiser Qualification Criteria,* the quantitative experience requirements must be satisfied by time spent on the appraisal process: analyzing factors that affect value; defining the problem; gathering and analyzing data; applying the appropriate analysis and methodology; and arriving at an opinion and correctly reporting the opinion in compliance with USPAP.

Based upon the minimum criteria set forth by the AQB, a state could, after review of your work log and work samples, grant you experience credit for work completed in ad valorem, mass appraisal assignments. However, check with the specific state appraiser regulatory agency in the jurisdiction in which you are seeking a credential to verify their requirements, which may be more restrictive.

Generic Experience Criteria and the STANDARDS

An applicant's experience must be in appraisal work conforming to STANDARDS 1, 2, 3, 4, 5, and/ or 6, where the appraiser demonstrates proficiency in appraisal principles, methodology, procedures (development), and reporting conclusions.

Documentation in the form of reports, certifications, or file memoranda, or, if such reports and memoranda are unavailable for good cause, other evidence at the credentialing authority's discretion that the work is compliant with USPAP must be provided as part of the state experience verification process to support the experience claimed.

The verification for experience credit claimed by an applicant shall be on forms prescribed by the state certification/licensing agency, which shall include:

- Type of property
- Date of report
- Address of appraised property
- Description of work performed by the trainee/applicant and scope of the review and supervision of the supervising appraiser
- Number of actual work hours by the trainee/applicant on the assignment
- The signature and state certification number of the supervising appraiser if applicable

Separate appraisal logs shall be maintained for each supervising appraiser, if applicable. There is **no maximum time limit** during which experience may be obtained.

√ **Note: Guide Note 6** within the Real Property Appraiser Qualification Criteria provides more information regarding the appraiser's log along with a sample illustration on page 79.

AQB Q&A #7

I am a trainee appraiser seeking a supervisory appraiser. I live in a state where appraisers are not required to be state-licensed or certified for appraisal assignments that do not involve federally-related transactions. I have found an appraiser that is willing to supervise my work and sign my appraisal experience log, but he does not possess a state license or certification. Would this individual qualify as my supervisory appraiser?

Response:

No, the *Real Property Appraiser Qualification Criteria* specifies supervisory appraisers shall be state-certified and in "good standing" in the jurisdiction in which the trainee appraiser practices for a period of at least three (3) years. The fact this individual is not a state-certified appraiser precludes this appraiser from acting as your supervisory appraiser and signing your appraisal experience log. However, be sure to check with your state appraiser regulatory agency to confirm the state's requirements, which could be more restrictive.

AQB Q&A #8

I am a trainee appraiser working towards my license. If I do not sign an appraisal report due to my company's policies or a client's assignment conditions, what verbiage is required in the report in order for the time I spent on the appraisal to count toward the experience requirements in the *Real Property Appraiser Qualification Criteria*?

Response:

If you provide significant real property appraisal assistance to a supervisory appraiser but do not sign the report certification, your supervisory appraiser <u>must</u> disclose that you provided significant real property appraisal assistance within the certification of the report. In addition, the supervisory appraiser must describe the extent of your assistance in the report (refer to the Uniform Standards of Professional Appraisal Practice [USPAP], Standards Rules 2-2 and 2-3, as well as Advisory Opinion 31, *Assignments Involving More Than One Appraiser*, for additional details).

Furthermore, the experience log you submit to your state appraiser regulatory agency must describe the work you performed in support of the hours of experience you claim for each assignment. Documentation in the form of reports, certifications, or file memoranda, or other evidence that the time you spent on the appraisal process is compliant with USPAP must be provided as part of the state experience verification process to support the experience claimed.

AQB Q&A #9

I am a supervisory appraiser and I hold a Certified General credential in two states: State A and State B. One of my trainees has a trainee appraiser's credential in State A only. I have an assignment in State B, and plan to take my trainee with me to work on the assignment. Will State A grant experience to my trainee appraiser for work performed in State B?

Response:

The *Real Property Appraiser Qualification Criteria* specifies experience must be gained under the supervision of the supervisory appraiser and the work must comply with USPAP. Thus, the *Real Property Appraiser Qualification Criteria* would not prohibit State A from granting the trainee appraiser credit in this case. However, be sure to check with the state appraiser regulatory agency in State A to confirm the state's requirements, which could be more restrictive.

AQB Q&A #10

I have been a Licensed Real Estate agent for several years and also a trainee appraiser for over one year. I have a supervisory appraiser for whom I perform appraisals and I also get paid by a bank to perform Broker Price Opinions (BPOs) that require very similar information as an appraisal (including providing six comps). I act as a completely unbiased person doing these BPOs and have no interest in the properties. Can these BPOs be counted on my appraisal experience log?

Response:

If the BPOs do not comply with USPAP, regardless of the level of detail or the scope of work performed, they are ineligible for experience credit. (Refer to USPAP for further information on not misrepresenting your role when acting as an appraiser versus a broker/sales person/mortgage broker.)

If, however, the development and reporting of the BPO complies with USPAP, and your supervisory appraiser provides direct supervision over your preparation thereof, reviews and signs your work product, it is possible a state appraiser regulatory agency might count these as appraisal experience. However, be sure to check with the specific state appraiser regulatory agency in the jurisdiction in which you are seeking a credential to verify their requirements, which may be more restrictive.

AQB Q&A #11

Is there an assumption that a typical residential appraisal takes "X" hours to develop and report? If someone submits a log to the state and says they have acquired 3,000 hours of experience by doing ten "URAR" form reports, would they be believed? Or, is there a range that makes sense, like between four and twelve hours for a "typical" assignment?

Response:

The *Real Property Appraiser Qualification Criteria* does not specify the amount of experience hours which may be claimed per assignment. The state appraiser regulatory agency in the jurisdiction where you are seeking a credential is responsible for examining your experience log and must be satisfied there is a reasonable relationship between the amounts of time you claim to have spent on an assignment and your description of work performed.

Some states have established typical hours for specific types of appraisal assignment types, which they use as a benchmark to identify potentially excessive experience claims. Be sure to check with your supervisory appraiser (if applicable) and your state appraiser regulatory agency to make sure you comply with the hourly requirements when claiming experience.

AQB Q&A #12

I am a trainee appraiser accumulating experience under a Certified Residential Supervisory appraiser. I understand that for my experience to be eligible for credit it must be performed with a certified appraiser; however, we occasionally receive assignments that I do not intend to use for experience credit. In assignments where I don't intend to claim experience credit, can I perform the assignment under the direction of a Licensed Residential appraiser, or even on my own without a supervisory appraiser?

Response:

No. Regardless of whether an assignment is being claimed for experience credit, a trainee appraiser must work under the direct supervision of a Certified Residential or Certified General appraiser. The *Real Property Appraiser Qualification Criteria* states:

The scope of practice for the Trainee Appraiser Classification is the appraisal of those properties which the **supervising certified appraiser** *is permitted by his/her current credential and that the supervising appraiser is qualified to appraise. (Bold added for emphasis.)*

Background Checks

All candidates for a real property appraiser credential must undergo background screening.

State appraiser regulatory agencies shall, at a minimum, obtain fingerprints of the individual, in digital form if practicable, and any appropriate identifying information for submission to the Federal Bureau of Investigation and/or any governmental agency or entity authorized to receive such information in connection with a state and national background check.

State appraiser regulatory agencies must ensure that all candidates for a real property appraiser credential do not possess a background that could call into question public trust.

State appraiser regulatory agencies must take proper steps to ensure those applicants found to possess a background which calls into question the applicant's ability to maintain public trust are not issued a real property appraiser credential.

State appraiser regulatory agencies shall not issue a real property appraiser credential if:

- The applicant has had an appraiser license or certification revoked in any governmental jurisdiction within the **five (5) year** period immediately preceding the date of application.

- The applicant has been convicted of, or pled guilty or *nolo contendere* to, a felony in a domestic, or foreign court (1) during the five (5) year period immediately preceding the date of the application for licensing or certification; or (2) at any time preceding the date of application, if such felony involved an act of fraud, dishonesty, or a breach of trust, or money laundering.

- The applicant has failed to demonstrate character and general fitness such as to command the confidence of the community and to warrant a determination that the appraiser will operate honestly, fairly, and efficiently within the purposes of the criteria.

Additional background issues that a state appraiser regulatory agency shall evaluate and consider prior to issuing (or taking disciplinary action against) a real property appraiser credential include, but are not limited to:

- Convictions of any criminal offense involving dishonesty, breach of trust, or money laundering against the individual or organizations controlled by the individual, or agreements to enter into a pretrial diversion or similar program in connection with the prosecution for such offense(s);

- Civil judicial actions against the individual in connection with financial services-related activities, dismissals with settlements, or judicial findings that the individual violated financial services-related statutes or regulations, except for actions dismissed without a settlement agreement;

- Actions or orders by a state or federal regulatory agency or foreign financial regulatory authority that:

  (1) Found the individual to have made a false statement or omission or been dishonest, unfair or unethical; to have been involved in a violation of a financial services-related regulation or statute; or to have been a cause of a financial services-related business having its authorization to do business denied, suspended, revoked, or restricted;

  (2) Are entered against the individual in connection with a financial services-related activity;

  (3) Denied, suspended, or revoked the individual's registration or license to engage in a financial services-related activity; disciplined the individual or otherwise by order prevented the individual from associating with a financial services-related business or restricted the individual activities; or

  (4) Barred the individual from association with an entity or its officers regulated by the agency or authority or from engaging in a financial services-related business;

- Final orders issued by a state or federal regulatory agency or foreign financial regulatory authority based on violations of any law or regulation that prohibits fraudulent, manipulative, or deceptive conduct;

- Revocation or suspension of the individual's authorization to act as an attorney, accountant, or state or federal contractor; and

- Customer-initiated financial services-related arbitration or civil action against the individual that required action, including settlements, or which resulted in a judgment.

Summary

1. The Appraisal Foundation establishes the minimum qualifying standards through its Appraiser Qualifications Board (AQB), while the state level adopts these standards and often adds additional qualifying standards. The Appraisal Standards Board (ASB) of The Appraisal Foundation (TAF) establishes the minimum standards of practice for appraisers, which are known as the Uniform Standards of Professional Appraisal Practice (USPAP).

2. There are four permitted appraiser classifications addressed the AQB: Appraiser Trainee, Licensed Residential Real Property Appraiser, Certified Residential Real Property Appraiser, and Certified General Real Property Appraiser.

3. All appraiser classifications must satisfactorily complete a minimum of 14 hours of appraiser continuing education during each year,

4. A supervisory appraiser must have been licensed as an appraiser or certified as a residential or general appraiser for at least three years. A supervisory appraiser must be in good standing for a minimum of three years. A supervisory appraiser's registration, certification, or license must not be currently subjected to discipline or practice restrictions.

5. For the Certified Residential Appraiser and Certified General Appraiser levels, a Bachelor's degree is required. The changes become effective at the national level January 1, 2015.

6. For the Licensed Residential Appraiser level, the candidate must have completed 30 semester hours of college-level education or possess an Associate's degree.

Chapter Quiz

1. *According to the Real Property Appraiser Qualification Criteria, which is a true statement regarding continuing education for appraisers when a jurisdiction observes a two-year continuing education cycle?*

   A. 14 hours must be completed in addition to the 7-hour USPAP Update course.

   B. 14 hours of continuing education in any topic must be completed.

   C. 28 hours of continuing education in any topic must be completed.

   D. 28 hours must be completed, which includes the 7-hour USPAP Update course.

2. *In order for attendees to receive continuing education credit hours, a continuing education course must be at least _____ in length.*

   A. 2 hours

   B. 4 hours

   C. 5 hours

   D. 7 hours

3. *When an appraiser credential candidate has successfully completed an AQB-approved qualifying examination, what period of time is allowed for the validity of the examination results?*

   A. 12 months

   B. 24 months

   C. 48 months

   D. 60 months

4. *Which is NOT required to be documented in a trainee's appraisal log?*

   A. address of appraised property

   B. date of report

   C. reporting option used

   D. type of property

5. *If a trainee assists a supervisory appraiser in an appraisal assignment, but does not sign the certification in the report, what procedure must be followed according to AQB criteria?*

   A. client must provide written consent allowing for the trainee's participation

   B. description of the extent of the assistance must be included in the report, with disclosure of the assistance included in the certification

   C. a statement must be included in the report with the reasoning for the trainee not signing the certification

   D. the trainee's participation in the report or the report certification should not be referenced

6. *An appraiser may serve as a supervisory appraiser, provided he or she has been in good standing with the jurisdiction in which a prospective trainee appraiser will practice for a minimum of what number of years?*

   A. 3 years

   B. 5 years

   C. 7 years

   D. 10 years

7. *Which statement regarding continuing education is NOT consistent with the Real Property Appraiser Qualification Criteria?*

   A. Appraisers are responsible to comply with the most recent version of USPAP from the date it becomes effective, regardless of when they complete the 7-Hour National USPAP Update Course.

   B. Credit may be awarded for a single state appraiser regulatory agency meeting per continuing education cycle.

   C. Excess continuing education hours earned during one CE cycle may be carried over and credited to the next CE cycle.

   D. For a partial year of 185 days within a continuing education cycle, no hours of continuing education are required.

8. *Practicum courses that are approved by the AQB Course Approval Program or state appraiser regulatory agencies can satisfy the non-traditional client experience requirement, which cannot exceed _____ of the total experience requirement.*

   A. 10%

   B. 25%

   C. 50%

   D. 75%

9. *The AQB's experience requirement must be satisfied by time spent on the appraisal process, be USPAP compliant, and be obtained after*

   A. January 30, 1989.

   B. December 31, 1992.

   C. April 1, 2005.

   D. January 1, 2008.

10. *The _____ ensures the financing for The Appraisal Foundation.*

    A. Appraisal Practices Board

    B. Appraiser Qualifications Board

    C. Appraisal Standards Board

    D. Board of Trustees

Chapter 2

Credentialing Requirements

In this chapter, specific credentialing requirements for supervisory and trainee appraisers will be introduced and explored. There are several credentialing requirements ranging from required education and examinations to experience hours and experience logs. A thorough understanding of all of the above is essential to successful appraiser training.

Helpful AQB Q&As will continue to appear to assist with understanding potentially confusing areas of the credentialing requirements.

Chapter Objectives

After completing this chapter, you will be able to:

- Identify specific qualifying requirements for supervisory appraisers and trainee appraisers.
- Identify the specific credentialing requirements for the appraiser classifications.

Supervisory Appraiser Requirements

While the significant change to appraiser qualification criteria focused upon the college education requirements mentioned earlier in the course, the 2015 Real Property Qualification Criteria also added specific supervisory appraiser requirements along with a mandate for specific supervisor appraiser/trainee appraiser coursework.

Those requirements along with the qualifying criteria for each appraiser classification will be addressed in this chapter. The following is applicable to the supervision of trainee appraisers.

Supervisory appraisers shall be responsible for the training, guidance, and direct supervision of the trainee appraiser by:

- Accepting responsibility for the appraisal by signing and certifying the appraisal complies with USPAP;

- Reviewing and signing the trainee appraiser appraisal report(s); and

- Personally inspecting each appraised property with the trainee appraiser until the supervisory appraiser determines the trainee appraiser is competent to inspect the property, in accordance with the COMPETENCY RULE of USPAP for the property type.

Supervisory appraisers shall be state-certified and in "good standing" in the jurisdiction in which the trainee appraiser practices for a period of **at least three (3) years**. In addition, supervisory appraisers shall **not** have been subject to any disciplinary action within any jurisdiction within **the last three (3) years** that affects the supervisory appraiser's legal eligibility to engage in appraisal practice. Finally, a supervisory appraiser subject to a disciplinary action would be considered to be in "good standing" **three (3) years *after*** the successful completion/termination of the sanction imposed against the appraiser.

Supervisory appraisers shall have been state-certified for a minimum of **three (3) years** prior to being eligible to become a supervisory appraiser. Supervisory appraisers must also comply with the COMPETENCY RULE of USPAP for the property type and geographic location in what the trainee appraiser is being supervised.

Whereas a trainee appraiser is permitted to have more than one supervisory appraiser, supervisory appraisers **may not supervise more than three (3) trainee appraisers at one time**, unless a state program in the credentialing jurisdiction provides for progress monitoring, supervisory certified appraiser qualifications, and supervision and oversight requirements for supervisory appraisers.

AQB Q&A #13

I am a state-certified appraiser who is also a supervisory appraiser. My state appraiser regulatory agency has levied a fine against me and required me to take an additional course. Is this considered a sanction that restricts the supervisory appraiser's "legal" eligibility to engage in appraisal practice?"

Response:

No. As long as the fine is paid and remedial education is completed and no further action is taken (probation or suspension), the supervisory appraiser could continue to supervise trainee appraisers. However, please check with your state appraiser regulatory agency, since it may adopt more stringent requirements.

AQB Q&A #14

Is a supervisory appraiser's eligibility to supervise trainee appraisers only evaluated when they initially become a supervisory appraiser, or is the supervisory appraiser's eligibility evaluated on an ongoing basis?

Response:

The supervisory appraiser's eligibility is evaluated on an ongoing basis. Thus, if any sanction is levied against a supervisory appraiser during the term of supervision that affects the supervisory appraiser's eligibility to practice, the supervisory appraiser would immediately lose the right to supervise trainee appraisers for the length of the sanction, plus an additional three years beyond the date the sanction is lifted.

AQB Q&A #15

I am a state-certified real property appraiser and I am supervising a trainee appraiser. I notice the *Real Property Appraiser Qualification Criteria* specifies supervisory appraisers shall not have been subject to any disciplinary action within any jurisdiction within the **last three (3) years** that affects the supervisory appraiser's legal eligibility to engage in appraisal practice. Can you provide examples of disciplinary actions that **would** affect my legal eligibility to engage in appraisal practice?

Response:

The AQB has interpreted a *disciplinary action* to mean any adverse, final, and non-appealable decision by a state regulatory, administrative, or judicial authority of competent jurisdiction, which affects an individual's *ability to practice*. Sanctions imposed may vary between jurisdictions and may consist of those that do **and** do not affect an appraiser's legal eligibility to practice.

Sanctions that **would** affect an appraiser's legal eligibility to engage in appraisal practice may include, but are not limited to:

- Any limitation preventing or restricting an appraiser from engaging in appraisal practice until a specified condition has been met.

- Any limitation preventing or restricting an appraiser from engaging in appraisal practice of specific property types for any duration of time.

- Suspension of a Certified General or Certified Residential credential in any jurisdiction.

- Revocation of a Certified General or Certified Residential credential in any jurisdiction.

√ **Caution!** Be sure to check with your state appraiser regulatory agency to confirm the state's requirements, which could be more restrictive.

AQB Q&A #16

Can you provide examples of disciplinary actions that **would not** affect my legal eligibility to engage in appraisal practice?

Response:

Sanctions that **would not** affect an appraiser's legal eligibility to engage in appraisal practice may include, but are not limited to:

- A monetary fine or penalty (without additional sanctions limiting the appraiser's legal eligibility to engage in appraisal practice).

- A letter of warning or reprimand.

- An educational requirement.

√ **Caution!** Be sure to check with your state appraiser regulatory agency to confirm the state's requirements, which could be more restrictive.

AQB Q&A #17

I am a state-certified real property appraiser in States A and B. I am also supervising a trainee appraiser in State A. I was recently investigated by the state board in State B for an alleged violation of USPAP and it was determined a violation was found to exist. Subsequently, State B suspended my appraiser certification for a period of **one (1) year**. Does this action preclude my continued supervision of the trainee appraiser in State A?

Response:

Yes, the *Real Property Appraiser Qualification Criteria* specifies supervisory appraisers shall not have been subject to any disciplinary action <u>within any jurisdiction</u> within the **last three (3) years** that affects the supervisory appraiser's legal eligibility to engage in appraisal practice. Although you may currently be in "good standing" in State A, your legal eligibility to engage in appraisal practice in State B has been suspended and you are no longer able to act as a supervisory appraiser in any jurisdiction until a **minimum of three (3) years** after the successful completion/termination of the sanction imposed against you. However, be sure to check with your state appraiser regulatory agency to confirm the state's requirements, which could be more restrictive.

AQB Q&A #18

I have been a Certified Residential appraiser for the **past five (5) years**. Last month, I was issued a Certified General credential in the same jurisdiction. Am I able to supervise a trainee appraiser working on commercial properties?

Response:

The *Real Property Appraiser Qualification Criteria* states supervisory appraisers shall be state-certified and in "good standing" in the jurisdiction in which the trainee appraiser practices for a period of **at least three (3) years**. The *Criteria* do not specify that a supervisory appraiser have a specific Certified Residential or Certified General credential, so you may be eligible to supervise a trainee appraiser performing commercial appraisals. However, the supervisory appraiser must comply with the COMPETENCY RULE of USPAP for the property type and geographic location the trainee appraiser is being supervised.

Experience Log

An appraisal experience log shall be maintained jointly by the supervisory appraiser and the trainee appraiser. It is the responsibility of **both** the supervisory appraiser and trainee appraiser to ensure the experience log is accurate, current, and complies with the requirements of the trainee appraiser's credentialing jurisdiction. (The minimum log requirements were presented earlier in Chapter 1 during the discussion of Experience Criteria.)

Supervisor Course Requirements

Supervisory appraisers shall be required to complete a course that, *at a minimum*, complies with the specifications for course content established by the AQB, which is specifically oriented to the requirements and responsibilities of supervisory appraisers and trainee appraisers.

The course is to be completed by the supervisory appraiser **prior to** supervising a trainee appraiser (and by trainee appraisers prior to obtaining a trainee credential). Obviously, the course you are now taking is intended to satisfy the requirement for completion of a course focused on the requirements and responsibilities of supervisory appraisers and trainee appraisers.

In terms of the AQB requirements for the course, both the trainee appraiser and supervisory appraiser shall be required to complete a course that, at a minimum, complies with the specifications for course content established by the AQB. The course will be oriented toward the requirements and responsibilities of supervisory appraisers and expectations for trainee appraisers. The course must be completed by the trainee appraiser prior to obtaining a Trainee Appraiser credential, and completed by the supervisory appraiser prior to supervising a trainee appraiser.

The AQB specifies that the course must achieve the following objectives:

- AQB minimum qualifications for becoming and remaining a supervisory appraiser or trainee appraiser.
- Jurisdictional credentialing requirements for supervisory appraisers and trainee appraisers that may exceed those of the criteria. (may be presented separately)
- Expectations and responsibilities of a trainee appraiser, or being a supervisory appraiser.
- Processes and roles of the entities involved in establishing qualifications for credentialed appraisers.
- Qualifications to become a credentialed appraiser.
- Basics of the Uniform Standards of Professional Appraisal Practice (USPAP).
- Responsibilities and requirements of a trainee appraiser's role, and a supervisory appraiser's role, in maintaining and signing all appropriate trainee appraiser experience logs.

AQB Q&A #19

I am currently a credentialed trainee appraiser. Am I required to take a supervisory appraiser and trainee appraiser course prior to January 1, 2015, in order to remain a trainee appraiser?

Response:

While the AQB encourages existing trainee appraisers to take the course, the 2015 *Real Property Appraiser Qualification Criteria* do not require currently-credentialed trainee appraisers to do so (i.e., you are "grandfathered" from the AQB's perspective). However, check with your state appraiser regulatory agency, since it may adopt more stringent requirements.

AQB Q&A #20

I am currently a supervisory appraiser of a trainee appraiser. Am I required to take a supervisory appraiser and trainee appraiser course prior to January 1, 2015, in order to continue to supervise trainee appraisers?

Response:

While the AQB encourages existing supervisory appraisers to take the course, the 2015 *Real Property Appraiser Qualification Criteria* do not require current supervisory appraisers to do so (i.e., you are "grandfathered" from the AQB's perspective). However, check with your state appraiser regulatory agency, since it may adopt more stringent requirements.

√ **Note:** If you seek to serve as a supervisory appraiser of any additional trainee appraiser(s) after the implementation date (e.g., January 1, 2015), you must fulfill all of the 2015 *Criteria* requirements to become a supervisory appraiser at that time.

Real Property Appraiser Classifications and Education

As mentioned earlier, there are four real property appraiser classifications recognized by the AQB:

1. Trainee appraiser
2. Licensed Residential Real Property Appraiser
3. Certified Residential Real Property Appraiser
4. Certified General Real Property Appraiser

Again, some jurisdictions do not offer credentials for all of these classifications, and some jurisdictions may reference a particular classification in a slightly different manner.

Reference may be made in the *Real Property Appraiser Qualification Criteria* and by some jurisdictions to an appraiser *designation*.

The use of the term *designation* must be interpreted in the proper context and not be confused as being the same as a voluntary designation offered by a professional appraiser organization. Licensing classifications may reference a designation in the context of alternative terminology used to describe a level of credential.

There are numerous professional appraiser organizations to which appraisers could voluntarily become members. Many of these organizations offer certain designations to denote specific levels of education, experience, or expertise of their respective members. Use of the term *designation* in any appraiser qualification criteria of the AQB or any jurisdiction is **not** referencing a designation offered by an appraiser trade organization.

AQB Q&A #21

I am a state-certified real property appraiser and I am supervising a trainee appraiser. I also carry a designation issued by a professional appraiser organization. I was recently investigated by my organization for an alleged violation of the organization's professional ethics requirements, and subsequently, my professional designation was revoked. Does a revocation of my designation by the professional organization preclude my continued supervision of the trainee appraiser?

Response:

No, the *Real Property Appraiser Qualification Criteria* specifies supervisory appraisers shall not have been subject to any disciplinary action within any jurisdiction within the **last three (3) years** that affects the supervisory appraiser's *legal eligibility* to engage in appraisal practice. Although your appraiser organization has imposed a disciplinary sanction by revoking your designation, this action does not, in and of itself, affect your legal eligibility to engage in appraisal practice in your credentialing jurisdiction. However, be sure to check with your state appraiser regulatory agency to confirm the state's requirements, which could be more restrictive.

Trainee Real Property Appraiser Classification

The Trainee Appraiser classification is intended to incorporate any documented non-certified/non-licensed real property appraisers who are subject to the *Real Property Appraiser Qualification Criteria*.

The AQB's criteria recognizes that individual credentialing jurisdictions may use different terminologies, which was just discussed.

"Trainee appraisers" include, but are not limited to:

- Registered appraisers
- Apprentice appraisers
- Provisional appraisers
- Other similar designations created by state appraiser regulatory agencies

The scope of practice for the trainee appraiser classification is the appraisal of those properties which the state-certified supervisory appraiser is permitted by his/her current credential and that the supervisory appraiser is competent to appraise.

The trainee appraiser, as well as the supervisory appraiser, shall be entitled to obtain copies of appraisal reports and/or permitted appropriate access and retrieval arrangements for all workfiles for appraisals in which he or she participated, in accordance with the RECORD KEEPING RULE of USPAP. In addition, all trainee appraisers must comply with the COMPETENCY RULE of USPAP for all assignments.

In terms of requirements for the trainee appraiser:

- There is **no examination** requirement for the trainee appraiser classification, but the trainee appraiser *shall pass the appropriate end-of-course examinations in all of the prerequisite courses* in order to earn credit for those courses.

- As the prerequisite for application, an applicant must have completed **75 creditable hours of qualifying education** as specified in the *Required Core Curriculum*.

- Additionally, applicants must pass the course examinations and pass the *15-Hour National USPAP Course* (or its AQB-approved equivalent) and examination as part of the 75 creditable hours.

- All qualifying education must be completed within the **five (5) year period prior to the date of submission** of a trainee appraiser application.

The Required Core Curriculum for the **Trainee Appraiser** classification includes:

Basic Appraisal Principles	30 Hours
Basic Appraisal Procedures	30 Hours
15-Hour National Uspap Course or Its Equivalent	15 Hours
Trainee Appraiser Education Requirements	**75 Hours**

√ **Note:** Jurisdictions often have greater requirements than the minimum Required Core Curriculum.

Experience and Training

Experience - No experience is required as a prerequisite for the Trainee Appraiser classification.

Training - The trainee appraiser shall be subject to direct control and supervision by a supervisory appraiser in good standing, who shall be state-certified.

- A trainee appraiser is permitted to have more than one supervisory appraiser.

- A supervisory appraiser may not supervise more than **three (3)** trainee appraisers, at one time, unless a program in the state appraiser regulatory jurisdiction provides for progress monitoring, supervising certified appraiser qualifications, and supervision and oversight requirements for supervisory appraisers.

Trainee Course Requirements

Trainee appraisers shall be required to complete a course that, *at minimum*, complies with the specifications for course content established by the AQB, which is specifically oriented to the requirements and responsibilities of supervisory appraisers and trainee appraisers. This is the same course as that required for supevisory appraisers, and was previously discussed.

- The course must be completed by the trainee appraiser prior to obtaining a trainee appraiser credential from the individual credentialing jurisdiction.

- The trainee appraiser course is **not eligible** towards the 75 hours of qualifying education required.

Trainee Appraiser Summary Matrix

Summary Matrix of the Trainee Real Property Appraiser Classification requirements:

	Curriculum (Core Courses)	College Requirements	Experience
Trainee Appraiser	• Basic Appraisal Principles (30 Hours) • Basic Appraisal Procedures (30 Hours) • 15-Hour National USPAP Course or its Equivalent (15 Hours) **Total Trainee Appraiser Education Requirements: 75 Hours**	• None	• None

Licensed Residential Real Property Appraiser Classification

The **Licensed Residential Real Property Appraiser** classification applies to the appraisal of:

- Non-complex one-to-four residential units having a transaction value less than $1,000,000.
- Complex one-to-four residential units having a transaction value less than $250,000.

Complex one-to-four unit residential property appraisal means *one in which the property to be appraised, the form of ownership, or the market conditions are atypical.* For non-federally related transaction appraisals, transaction value shall mean market value.

The classification includes the appraisal of vacant or unimproved land that is utilized for one-to-four residential units, or for which the highest and best use is for one-to-four residential units. The classification does **not** include the appraisal of subdivisions for which a development analysis/appraisal is necessary.

√ **Note:** All Licensed Residential Real Property Appraisers must comply with the COMPETENCY RULE of USPAP.

The AQB-approved Licensed Residential Real Property Appraiser examination must be successfully completed. The prerequisites for taking the AQB-approved examination are completion of:

- **One hundred fifty (150) creditable class hours** as specified in the *Required Core Curriculum*
- Completion of the college-level education requirements specified in by the criteria
- **Two thousand (2,000) hours of qualifying experience** in no fewer than **twelve (12) months**.

The Required Core Curriculum for the **Licensed Residential Appraiser** classification includes:

Basic Appraisal Principles	30 Hours
Basic Appraisal Procedures	30 Hours
15-Hour National Uspap Course or Its Equivalent	15 Hours
Residential Market Analysis and Highest and Best Use	15 Hours
Residential Appraiser Site Valuation and Cost Approach	15 Hours
Residential Sales Comparison and Income Approaches	30 Hours
Residential Report Writing and Case Studies	15 Hours
Licensed Residential Education Requirements	**150 Hours**

As part of the 150 required hours, the applicant shall successfully complete the *15-Hour National USPAP Course*, or its AQB-approved equivalent, and the examination.

There is no alternative to successful completion of the USPAP Course and examination.

√ **Note:** Jurisdictions often have greater requirements than the minimum Required Core Curriculum.

College Education Requirement

Applicants for the **Licensed Residential credential** shall successfully complete *30 semester hours of college-level education*, from an accredited college, junior college, community college, or university. The college or university must be a degree-granting institution accredited by the Commission on Colleges, a regional or national accreditation association, or by an accrediting agency that is recognized by the U.S. Secretary of Education. If an accredited college or university accepts the College-Level Examination Program® (CLEP) and examination(s) and issues a transcript for the exam, showing its approval, it will be considered as credit for the college course.

For college -level courses taken in a quarterly system versus a semester system, one quarter hour credit is equivalent to **.67 semester credit hours**. Conversely, one semester credit hour is equivalent to **1.5 quarter credit hours**.

For example, to satisfy the 30 semester credit hour requirement for the Licensed Residential Real Property Appraiser classification, an applicant needs to successfully pass those applicable courses that generate 45 quarter credit hours, (i.e., 30 semester credit hours x 1.5 conversion factor).

Applicants holding an *Associate degree, or higher,* from an accredited college, junior college, community college, or university satisfy the 30-hour college-level education requirement. As a side note, applicants with a college degree from a foreign country may have their education evaluated, based upon the "equivalency" guidelines contained in the criteria.

Upgrading Classifications

Appraisers holding a valid trainee appraiser credential may satisfy the educational requirements for the **Licensed Residential Real Property Appraiser** credential by completing the following additional educational hours:

Residential Market Analysis and Highest and Best Use	15 Hours
Residential Appraiser Site Valuation and Cost Approach	15 Hours
Residential Sales Comparison and Income Approaches	30 Hours
Residential Report Writing and Case Studies	15 Hours
TOTAL	**75 Hours**

Trainee appraisers wishing to change to the Licensed Residential Real Property Appraiser classification must also satisfy the college-level education requirements.

Licensed Residential Appraiser Summary Matrix

Summary Matrix of the Licensed Residential Real Property Appraiser Classification requirements:

	Curriculum (Core Courses)	College Requirements	Experience
Licensed Residential Appraiser*	• Basic Appraisal Principles (30 Hours) • Basic Appraisal Procedures (30 Hours) • 15-Hour National USPAP Course or its Equivalent (15 Hours) • Residential Market Analysis and Highest and Best Use (15 Hours) • Residential Appraiser Site Valuation and Cost Approach (15 Hours) • Residential Sales Comparison and Income Approaches (30 Hours) • Residential Report Writing and Case Studies (15 Hours) **Total Licensed Residential Appraiser Requirements: 150 Hours**	• 30 semester credit hours of college-level education from an accredited college, junior college, community college, or university; OR an Associate's degree or higher (in any field).	• 2,000 hours of experience in no fewer than 12 months.

AQB Q&A #22

I am a Licensed Residential appraiser and I have been asked to appraise a home on 40 acres in a marketplace where there are no other home sites larger than 5 acres. The appraisal is being requested by a federally-chartered bank in order to evaluate the subject property as collateral for a $1.5 million mortgage loan. Does my Licensed Residential credential permit me to appraise this property?

Response:

No. The scope of practice for the Licensed Residential classification allows for appraisals of "complex" 1-4 unit residential properties up to a transaction value of $250,000, and it appears this assignment would qualify as "complex." However, even if it does not qualify as "complex," the Licensed Residential classification only allows for appraisals of "non-complex" 1-4 unit residential properties up to a transaction value of $1 million. Therefore, this property could not be appraised by a Licensed Residential appraiser to support a federally-related transaction (FRT). If this appraisal was not being performed for a FRT, and you could do so in compliance with the COMPETENCY RULE and all other provisions of USPAP, then check with your state appraiser regulatory agency to see if the state permits you to value a property with these characteristics.

Certified Residential Real Property Appraiser Classification

The **Certified Residential Real Property Appraiser** classification qualifies the appraiser to appraise one-to-four residential units without regard to value or complexity.

- The classification includes the appraisal of vacant or unimproved land that is utilized for one-to-four residential units purposes or for which the highest and best use is for one-to-four residential units.

- The classification does **not** include the appraisal of subdivisions for which a development analysis/appraisal is necessary.

√ **Caution!** All Certified Residential appraisers must comply with the COMPETENCY RULE of USPAP.

The AQB-approved Certified Residential Real Property Appraiser examination must be successfully completed. The prerequisites for taking the AQB-approved examination are completion of:

- **Two hundred (200) creditable class hours** as specified in the *Required Core Curriculum*
- Completion of the college-level education requirements specified in the criteria.
- **Two thousand five hundred (2,500) hours** of qualifying experience obtained in no fewer than **twenty-four (24) months**.

The Required Core Curriculum for the **Certified Residential Appraiser** classification includes:

Basic Appraisal Principles	30 Hours
Basic Appraisal Procedures	30 Hours
15-Hour National Uspap Course or Its Equivalent	15 Hours
Residential Market Analysis and Highest and Best Use	15 Hours
Residential Appraiser Site Valuation and Cost Approach	15 Hours
Residential Sales Comparison and Income Approaches	30 Hours
Residential Report Writing and Case Studies	15 Hours
Statistics, Modeling And Finance	15 Hours
Advanced Residential Applications and Case Studies	15 Hours
Appraisal Subject Matter Electives*	
*(May Include Hours Over Minimum Shown Above In Other Modules)	20 Hours
Certified Residential Education Requirements	**200 Hours**

As part of the 200 required hours, the applicant shall successfully complete the *15-Hour National USPAP Course*, or its AQB-approved equivalent, and the examination. **There is no alternative to successful completion of the USPAP Course and examination.**

√ **Note:** Jurisdictions often have greater requirements than the minimum Required Core Curriculum.

College Education

Applicants for the **Certified Residential** credential must hold *a Bachelor's degree, or higher*, from an accredited college or university. The college or university must be a degree-granting institution accredited by the Commission on Colleges, a national or regional accreditation association, or by an accrediting agency that is recognized by the U.S. Secretary of Education. Trainee appraisers and Licensed Residential Real Property Appraisers wishing to change to the Certified Residential Real Property Appraiser classification must also satisfy the college degree requirements.

√ **Note:** Applicants with a college degree from a foreign country may have their education evaluated, based upon the "equivalency" guidelines contained in the criteria.

Upgrading Classifications

Appraisers holding a valid Trainee Appraiser credential may satisfy the educational requirements for the **Certified Residential Real Property Appraiser** credential by completing the following additional educational hours:

Residential Market Analysis and Highest and Best Use	15 Hours
Residential Appraiser Site Valuation and Cost Approach	15 Hours
Residential Sales Comparison and Income Approaches	30 Hours
Residential Report Writing and Case Studies	15 Hours
Statistics, Modeling and Finance	15 Hours
Advanced Residential Applications and Case Studies	15 Hours
Appraisal Subject Matter Electives	20 Hours
TOTAL	**125 Hours**

Appraisers holding a valid Licensed Residential Real Property Appraiser credential may satisfy the educational requirements for the **Certified Residential Real Property Appraiser** credential by completing the following additional educational hours:

Statistics, Modeling and Finance	15 Hours
Advanced Residential Applications and Case Studies	15 Hours
Appraisal Subject Matter Electives	20 Hours
TOTAL	**50 Hours**

Trainee appraisers and Licensed Residential Real Property Appraisers wishing to change to the Certified Residential Real Property Appraiser classification must also satisfy the college-level education requirements.

Certified Residential Appraiser Summary Matrix

Summary Matrix of the Certified Residential Real Property Appraiser Classification requirements

	Curriculum (Core Courses)	College Requirements	Experience
Certified Residential Appraiser	• Basic Appraisal Principles (30 Hours) • Basic Appraisal Procedures (30 Hours) • 15-Hour National USPAP Course or its Equivalent (15 Hours) • Residential Market Analysis and Highest and Best Use (15 Hours) • Residential Appraiser Site Valuation and Cost Approach (15 Hours) • Residential Sales Comparison and Income Approaches (30 Hours) • Residential Report Writing and Case Studies (15 Hours) • Statistics, Modeling, and Finance (15 Hours) • Advanced Residential Applications and Case Studies (15 Hours) • Appraisal Subject Matter Electives (May include hours over minimum shown above in other modules) (20 Hours) **Total Certified Residential Appraiser Requirements: 200 Hours**	• Bachelor's degree or higher (in any field) from an accredited college or university.	• 2,500 hours of experience in no fewer than 24 months.

AQB Q&A #23

I hold a Licensed Residential credential and plan to upgrade to a Certified Residential credential. What courses do I need to take?

Response:

The additional *Required Core Curriculum* coursework required of those appraisers holding a valid Licensed Residential credential are as follows: *Statistics, Modeling & Finance* (15 hours), *Advanced Residential Applications and Case Studies* (15 hours) and *Appraisal Subject Matter Electives* (20 hours).

In addition to the *Required Core Curriculum* requirements, candidates must also meet the college degree, experience, and examination requirements for the Certified Residential credential. Applicants for the Certified Residential credential must hold a Bachelor's degree from an accredited college or university. The minimum experience requirement **is 2,500 hours** obtained during not less than **twenty-four (24) months**. The AQB-approved Certified Residential Real Property Appraiser Examination must also be successfully completed.

Certified General Real Property Appraiser Classification

The **Certified General Real Property Appraiser** classification qualifies the appraiser to appraise **all** types of real property.

√ **Note:** All Certified General appraisers must comply with the COMPETENCY RULE of USPAP.

The AQB-approved Certified General Real Property Appraiser examination must be successfully completed. The prerequisites for taking the AQB-approved examination are completion of:

- **Three hundred (300) creditable class hours** as specified in the *Required Core Curriculum*
- Completion of the college-level education requirements specified in the criteria.
- **Three thousand (3,000) hours** of qualifying experience obtained in no fewer than **thirty (30) months**, where a minimum of **one thousand five hundred (1,500) hours must be obtained in non-residential appraisal work.**

The Required Core Curriculum for the **Certified General Appraiser** classification includes:

Basic Appraisal Principles	30 Hours
Basic Appraisal Procedures	30 Hours
15-Hour National Uspap Course or Its Equivalent	15 Hours
General Appraiser Market Analysis and Highest and Best Use	30 Hours
Statistics, Modeling and Finance	15 Hours
General Appraiser Sales Comparison Approach	30 Hours
General Appraiser Site Valuation and Cost Approach	30 Hours
General Appraiser Income Approach	60 Hours
General Appraiser Report Writing and Case Studies	30 Hours
Appraisal Subject Matter Electives*	
*(May Include Hours Over Minimum Shown Above In Other Modules)	30 Hours
Certified General Education Requirements	**300 Hours**

Applicants must demonstrate that their education includes the core courses listed in these criteria, with **particular emphasis on non-residential properties. Residential** is defined as "*composed of one-to-four residential units.*"

√ **Note:** Jurisdictions often have greater requirements than the minimum Required Core Curriculum.

College Education

Applicants for the **Certified General credential** must hold *a Bachelor's degree or higher* from an accredited college or university.

The college or university must be a degree-granting institution accredited by the Commission on Colleges, a national or regional accreditation association, or by an accrediting agency that is recognized by the U.S. Secretary of Education.

Applicants with a college degree from a foreign country may have their education evaluated, based upon the "equivalency" guidelines contained in the criteria.

Upgrading Classifications

Appraisers holding a valid trainee appraiser credential may satisfy the educational requirements for the **Certified General Real Property Appraiser** credential by completing the following additional educational hours:

General Appraiser Market Analysis and Highest and Best Use	30 Hours
Statistics, Modeling and Finance	15 Hours
General Appraiser Sales Comparison Approach	30 Hours
General Appraiser Site Valuation and Cost Approach	30 Hours
General Appraiser Income Approach	60 Hours
General Appraiser Report Writing and Case Studies	30 Hours
Appraisal Subject Matter Electives	30 Hours
TOTAL	**225 Hours**

Appraisers holding a valid **Licensed Residential Real Property Appraiser** credential may satisfy the educational requirements for the Certified General Real Property Appraiser credential by completing the following additional educational hours:

General Appraiser Market Analysis and Highest and Best Use	15 Hours
Statistics, Modeling and Finance	15 Hours
General Appraiser Sales Comparison Approach	15 Hours
General Appraiser Site Valuation and Cost Approach	15 Hours
General Appraiser Income Approach	45 Hours
General Appraiser Report Writing and Case Studies	15 Hours
Appraisal Subject Matter Electives	30 Hours
TOTAL	**150 Hours**

Appraisers holding a valid **Certified Residential Real Property Appraiser** credential may satisfy the educational requirements for the Certified General Real Property Appraiser credential by completing the following additional educational hours:

General Appraiser Market Analysis and Highest and Best Use	15 Hours
General Appraiser Sales Comparison Approach	15 Hours
General Appraiser Site Valuation and Cost Approach	15 Hours
General Appraiser Income Approach	45 Hours
General Appraiser Report Writing and Case Studies	10 Hours
TOTAL	**100 Hours**

Trainee Appraisers, Licensed Residential Real Property Appraisers, and Certified Residential Real Property Appraisers wishing to change to the Certified General Real Property Appraiser classification must also satisfy the college-level education requirements for certified general appraisers.

Certified General Real Property Appraiser Summary Matrix

Summary Matrix of the Certified General Real Property Appraiser Classification requirements

	Curriculum (Core Courses)	College Requirements	Experience
Certified General Appraiser	• Basic Appraisal Principles (30 Hours) • Basic Appraisal Procedures (30 Hours) • 15-Hour National USPAP Course or its Equivalent (15 Hours) • General Appraiser Market Analysis and Highest and Best Use (30 Hours) • Statistics, Modeling, and Finance (15 Hours) • General Appraiser Sales Comparison Approach (30 Hours) • General Appraiser Site Valuation and Cost Approach (30 Hours) • General Appraiser Income Approach (60 Hours) • General Appraiser Report Writing and Case Studies (30 Hours) • Appraisal Subject Matter Electives (May include hours over minimum shown above in other modules) (30 Hours) **Total Certified General Appraiser Requirements: 300 Hours**	• Bachelor's degree or higher (in any field) from an accredited college or university.	• 3,000 hours in no fewer than 30 months (of which 1,500 hours must be in non-residential appraisal work).

*Trainee Appraisers, Licensed Residential Real Property Appraisers, and Certified Residential Real Property Appraisers wishing to change to the Certified General Real Property Appraiser classification must also satisfy the college-level education requirement for certified general appraisers.

**Trainees must complete required supervisory and trainee course prior to gaining experience.

AQB Q&A #24

I hold a Certified Residential credential and now I plan to pursue a Certified General credential. The *Criteria* indicate I am required to successfully complete **100** additional hours of qualifying education. Will these additional hours make me qualified to pass the National Uniform Licensing and Certification Examination for the Certified General classification?

Response:

The National Uniform Licensing and Certification Examination for the Certified General classification is based upon the **300** hours of *Required Core Curriculum* coursework as outlined in the *Real Property Appraiser Qualification Criteria*. Depending upon when you completed your original education and the nature of your practice, you may be able to pass the National General Certification Exam. However, the AQB urges you to examine the *Required Core Curriculum* to identify any possible areas of perceived weakness in your education, and prepare yourself by taking additional qualifying education courses in those areas.

AQB Q&A #25

I hold a Certified Residential credential and I am pursuing a Certified General credential in the same jurisdiction. Does the AQB require any supervised experience to upgrade from a Certified Residential appraiser to a Certified General appraiser?

Response:

The *Real Property Appraiser Qualification Criteria* does not specifically address a formal Supervisory appraiser relationship for Certified or Licensed appraisers seeking an upgrade to their credential. However, you must comply with the COMPETENCY RULE of USPAP when you obtain your non-residential property experience, which may require that you work with an existing Certified General appraiser who is competent in the property type and geographic area. Be sure to check with the state appraiser regulatory agency in the state where you plan to seek the credential to confirm the state's requirements, as states may implement more stringent requirements.

AQB Q&A #26

I am presently a Certified Residential appraiser and I am pursuing a change to Certified General. I realize a trainee who applies to become Certified General is required to accumulate 3,000 hours of experience (with at least 1,500 being non-residential). However, does this mean that a Certified Residential appraiser would only have to accumulate 1,500 hours of commercial experience to satisfy the experience requirement?

Response:

The *Real Property Appraiser Qualification Criteria* require 3,000 hours of experience accumulated during no fewer than 30 months, of which 1,500 hours must be non-residential. Under the *Criteria*, experience gained in pursuit of a credential is not exclusive to that specific credential. Thus, based upon the minimum criteria set forth by the AQB, a state appraiser regulatory agency could, after review, count the experience earned toward your Certified Residential credential along with additional experience earned toward the 3,000-hour requirement for the Certified General credential. However, be sure to check with the specific state appraiser regulatory agency in the jurisdiction in which you are seeking a credential to verify their requirements, which may be more restrictive.

AQB Q&A #27

I received my Certified Residential appraiser credential in 2004, and now I would like to get my Certified General credential. According to my state appraiser regulatory agency, because I did not satisfy the qualifying educational requirements for the Certified General credential prior to January 1, 2015, I am required to start from the beginning and complete all the qualifying education required for a Certified General credential. I am told this even includes the classes I originally took to get my Certified Residential credential (e.g. *Basic Appraisal Principles* and *Basic Appraisal Procedures*). Is this correct?

Response:

Per the *Real Property Appraiser Qualification Criteria*, appraisers holding a valid Certified Residential appraiser credential may satisfy the educational requirements for the Certified General appraiser credential by completing the following additional educational hours: *General Appraiser Market Analysis and Highest and Best Use* (15 hours); *General Appraiser Sales Comparison Approach* (15 hours); *General Appraiser Site Valuation and Cost Approach* (15 hours); *General Appraiser Income Approach* (45 hours); and *General Appraiser Report Writing and Case Studies* (15 hours).

The noted 100 total hours of additional qualifying education is the minimum that must be completed. In addition, you will need to satisfy the college degree requirement, complete the additional hours of experience, and successfully complete the National Uniform Licensing and Certification exam for the Certified General classification. As with all of the *Criteria* established by the AQB, states may create requirements that are greater than those established by the AQB. As a result, you will need to check with your state appraiser regulatory agency to determine the exact requirements to change your credential.

The AQB National Appraiser Examination

Supervisory appraisers and trainee appraisers must be mindful through the education and experience process of the preparedness necessary for the trainee to successfully pass the AQB National Appraiser Examination.

To be **licensed or certified as an appraiser**, the applicant must pass an examination that is appropriate for the classification applied for and possess:

- Knowledge of technical terms commonly used in real estate appraisal.

- An understanding of the principles of land economics, real estate appraisal processes, reliable sources of appraising data, and problems likely to be encountered in the gathering, interpreting, and processing of data in carrying out appraisal disciplines.

- An understanding of the standards for the development and communication of real estate appraisals.

- Knowledge of theories of depreciation, cost estimating, methods of capitalization, and the mathematics of real estate appraisal.

The passing score for the national uniform examination is determined by the AQB. The candidate must receive a **scaled score of 75 or greater**. A scaled score of 75 is **not** to be interpreted as 75% of the questions were answered correctly.

Scaled scores can range from **0 to 150**. The scaled scores are computed from raw scores. Raw scores, or percentage scores, are the actual number of questions answered correctly. Raw scores are mathematically converted to scaled scores to maintain a consistency in the meaning of scores, regardless of when the examination was taken or the difficulty of the examination.

AQB Q&A #28

Under the 2015 *Real Property Appraiser Qualification Criteria*, I understand that all education and experience must be completed and approved prior to taking the National Uniform Licensing and Certification Examination. Once I pass the examination, within what time period must I submit the application for my credential?

Response:

Examination results are valid for **24 months**. If your state appraiser regulatory agency has a separate post-examination application (i.e., you are not awarded the credential "automatically" by virtue of successfully passing the examination) you would need to submit your complete application within 24 months of successful completion of the exam. You should be sure to check with your state appraiser regulatory agency to determine when your application must be submitted.

Chapter Summary

1. Integral, to the AQB 2015 qualifying standards, is the requirement for supervisory appraisers and trainee appraisers to complete specific coursework focused on the topic of the requirements and responsibilities of supervisory appraisers and expectations for trainee appraisers. The course must be completed by the trainee appraiser prior to obtaining a trainee appraiser credential, and completed by the supervisory appraiser prior to supervising a trainee appraiser.

2. The Appraiser Trainee level has no experience requirement. To be qualified to apply for a Licensed Residential Appraiser credential, the candidate must complete 2,000 hours of real property appraisal experience obtained over not less than a 12-month period. To be qualified to apply for a Certified Residential Appraiser credential, the candidate must complete 2,500 hours of real property appraisal experience obtained over not less than a 24-month period. For Certified General Appraiser candidates, they must complete 3,000 hours of real property appraisal experience obtained over not less than a 30-month period.

3. All experience claimed for all licensure classifications must be obtained after January 30, 1989, and must be USPAP compliant. For the certified general appraiser, at least 50% (1,500 hours) of the claimed experience must be in nonresidential appraisal work. The 50% requirement mirrors the requirement of the AQB.

4. Experience shall be accounted for on an appraisal experience log.

5. The passing score for the national uniform examination as determined by the AQB of The Appraisal Foundation is a scaled score of 75 or greater. A scaled score does not refer to a percentage.

6. Supervisory appraisers must accept responsibility for all elements of the assignment and the appraisal report by signing and certifying the report is in compliance with USPAP; reviewing the appraiser trainee appraisal reports; and personally inspecting each appraised property with the appraiser trainee until the trainee is competent.

7. A registered trainee appraiser is permitted to have more than one supervisory appraiser. A supervising appraiser may not supervise more than three (3) registered trainee appraisers at one time.

Chapter Quiz

1. *How many classroom hours of core curriculum courses must a candidate complete in order to satisfy the requirements for the Appraiser Trainee classification?*

   A. 15
   B. 25
   C. 75
   D. 100

2. *Given no stricter jurisdictional requirement, supervisory appraisers must personally inspect each appraised property with the trainee appraiser*

   A. for a period of at least 6 months, but no longer than one year.
   B. through at least the time that 50% of the trainee's experience requirement has been earned.
   C. until the supervisory appraiser determines the trainee is competent to do so on their own.
   D. whenever it is practical for the supervisory appraiser to do so.

3. *The Supervisory Appraiser's eligibility to supervise Trainee Appraisers is evaluated*

   A. at the time the supervision commenced.
   B. at the end of each year.
   C. on an ongoing basis.
   D. twice annually by each applicable jurisdiction.

4. *Appraiser Trainee applicants must ensure that all qualifying education submitted with an application for the credential must have been completed within _____ years prior to the date of the submission.*

   A. 2
   B. 3
   C. 5
   D. 7

5. *According to the AQB requirements, in addition to completion of the core education requirements, Appraiser Trainee candidates must also*

   A. be screened for presence of illegal drugs by the FBI.
   B. have performed at least 2,000 hours of appraisal experience.
   C. pass the appropriate end-of-course examinations for the core courses.
   D. successfully pass an AQB-approved credentialing examination.

6. *Within their total requirement, candidates for the Certified General Real Property Appraiser classification must accumulate at least _____ hours of non-residential appraisal experience.*

   A. 1,500
   B. 2,000
   C. 2,500
   D. 3,000

7. *Which would NOT be a sanction that would affect an appraiser's legal eligibility to engage in appraisal practice?*

   A. Letter of warning or reprimand, or an imposed educational requirement as a result of disciplinary action.
   B. Limitation preventing or restricting an appraiser from engaging in appraisal practice of specific property types for any duration of time.
   C. Limitation preventing or restricting an appraiser from engaging in appraisal practice until a specified condition has been met.
   D. Suspension or revocation of a Certified Residential or Certified General credential in any jurisdiction.

8. *If a supervisory appraiser holds credentials in two states and his credential is suspended in one of the states, may he or she continue to supervise in the state for which his credential is still valid?*

   A. No, a supervising appraiser must be in good standing in all jurisdictions in which they hold a credential.
   B. No, not unless the suspending state allows a special provision.
   C. Yes, suspension in one state does not affect the ability to supervise in another state.
   D. Yes, the AQB specifically allows an exemption if the remaining state is still in good standing.

9. *Although it could vary by jurisdiction, the AQB specifies that candidates for the Licensed Residential Appraiser classification must complete 2,000 of qualifying experience in a period of not less than*

   A. 12 months.
   B. 20 months.
   C. 24 months.
   D. 30 months.

10. *Appraisers holding a valid Trainee Appraiser credential may satisfy the educational requirements for the Certified Residential Real Property Appraiser credential by completing _____ additional core education hours.*

   A. 75
   B. 100
   C. 125
   D. 200

Chapter 3

Supervisors, Trainees, and USPAP

Now that various national and jurisdictional qualification regulations for appraisers have been discussed, we will turn our focus to the standards of appraisal practice – USPAP. Specifically, our discussion will be concentrated upon the Rules and obligations applicable when an individual is acting as an appraiser, along with the applicable Rules serving as guidelines for developing and communicating a real property appraisal. Also illustrated, will be relevant USPAP Frequently Asked Questions (FAQ) and USPAP Advisory Opinions. It is important to remember that FAQs and Advisory Opinions are not part of USPAP, but are included with USPAP as addenda to offer guidance.

It could be certainly argued that in-depth knowledge and compliance with USPAP is paramount in the responsibilities of supervisory appraisers and trainees. Supervisory appraisers must ensure that the trainee is in compliance, while the trainee appraiser has the responsibility to comply with USPAP and ensure the directions and actions of their supervisory appraiser are compliant, as well. Whereas appraiser qualifications are the product of the Appraisal Qualifications Board (AQB), USPAP and elements related to it are the product of the Appraisal Standards Board (ASB).

Chapter Objectives

After completing this chapter, you will be able to:

- Specify the obligations of the ETHICS RULE and RECORD KEEPING RULE of USPAP and how they relate to supervisory appraisers and trainee appraisers.

- Describe the obligations of the COMPETENCY RULE and the SCOPE OF WORK RULE and how they relate to supervisory appraisers and trainee appraisers.

Appraiser's Peers Other appraisers who have expertise and competency in a similar type of assignment. *

Assignment Results An appraiser's opinions and conclusions developed specific to an assignment. *

Confidential Information Information that is either identified by the client as confidential when providing it to an appraiser and that is not available from any other source; or classified as confidential or private by applicable law or regulation.*

Scope of Work The type and extent of research and analyses in an appraisal or appraisal review assignment.*

Workfile Documentation necessary to support an appraiser's analyses, opinions, and conclusions. *

*USPAP 2016-2017 Edition

Key Terms

Appraisal Standards Board

The **Appraisal Standards Board (ASB)**:

- Establishes, improves, and promulgates USPAP.
- Is responsible for the subject, style, content, and substance of USPAP and other communications related to appraisal standards, including Advisory Opinions and FAQs.
- Writes periodic Q&As in response to questions received regarding USPAP.
- Issues exposure drafts for public comment of proposed changes to USPAP.

> *Applicable USPAP Rules*
>
> The ETHICS RULE and the COMPETENCY RULE of USPAP (as well as the JURISDICTIONAL EXCEPTION RULE) are applicable to **all appraisal practice**. In other words, these rules are applicable *any time one is acting as an appraiser*, not just when an appraiser is performing an appraisal or appraisal review.
>
> The RECORD KEEPING RULE and the SCOPE OF WORK RULE of USPAP apply *only when an appraiser is performing an appraisal or appraisal review*.

Overview of the ETHICS RULE

Core standards of professional behavior are contained in the ETHICS RULE. The ETHICS RULE sets forth foundational obligations when acting in the role of an appraiser and amplifies that an appraiser is required to always observe the highest standards of professional ethics.

Inherent within this requirement are general obligations for appraisers to:

- Not misrepresent their role when providing a valuation service that is outside of appraisal practice.
- Perform in compliance with USPAP when required by law regulation or agreement.
- Certify compliance with USPAP.
- Not communicate in a manner that is misleading.

The ETHICS RULE is applicable to an appraiser's conduct in general, as well as to development and communication issues and commences by reciting a foundational obligation:

*An appraiser must **promote and preserve the public trust inherent in appraisal practice** by observing the highest standards of professional ethics.*

The ETHICS RULE consists of three sections:

- Conduct
- Management
- Confidentiality

These sections of the ETHICS RULE are applicable to all appraisal practice.

Conduct Section

Obligations of the <u>Conduct</u> section of the ETHICS RULE regarding **general conduct** include:

- Appraisers must not engage in criminal conduct.
- Appraisers must always be impartial, objective, and independent, without accommodating personal interests.
- Appraisers must perform in compliance with USPAP.
- Appraisers must not willfully or knowingly violate the requirements of the RECORD KEEPING RULE.

Obligations of the <u>Conduct</u> section of the ETHICS RULE regarding **development issues** include:

- Appraisers must not perform an assignment with bias.
- Appraisers must not advocate for the cause or interest of any party or issue.
- Appraisers must not accept assignments that include reporting predetermined opinions and conclusions.
- Appraisers must not misrepresent their role when providing valuation services outside of appraisal practice.
- Appraisers must not perform assignments in a grossly negligent manner.
- Appraisers must not use or rely on unsupported conclusions regarding characteristics related to specifically recognized protected classes.
- In the same regard, they must not rely upon unsupported conclusions indicating that homogeneity of such characteristics is necessary to maximize value.

Protected classes or related characteristics of those classes that are indicated in USPAP include:

- Race
- Color
- Religion
- National origin
- Gender
- Marital status
- Familial status
- Age
- Receipt of public assistance income
- Handicap

Next, examining the obligations of the <u>Conduct</u> section of the ETHICS RULE regarding **communication issues,** appraisers must not:

- Communicate **assignment results**, *an appraiser's opinions and conclusions developed specific to an assignment*, with the intent to mislead or defraud.
- Communicate, use, or allow an employee or others to use a fraudulent or misleading report.

The following information must be disclosed to the client if known prior to accepting an assignment, or if discovered at any time during an assignment:

- Any current or prospective interest in a subject property or the parties involved in the assignment
- Any services as an appraiser, or in any other capacity, regarding the subject property performed within a **three-year period prior** to acceptance of the assignment

In addition to the disclosure made prior to accepting an assignment or one made if discovered any time during an assignment, **disclosure must be made in the certification** of each subsequent report. Disclosing this information is important to preserving public trust, and it gives the client an opportunity to evaluate the information *before* engaging the appraiser.

√ **Caution!** If the appraiser has agreed with a client in a previous assignment to not disclose that he or she performed that appraisal, the appraiser must decline all assignments that fall within the three-year period.

Management Section of ETHICS RULE

The <u>Management</u> section of the ETHICS RULE addresses, in part:

- Disclosing fees, commissions, or things of value paid in connection with the procurement of an assignment.

- Unacceptable assignment conditions and compensation arrangements.

- Advertising/soliciting assignments in a false, misleading, or exaggerated manner.

- Affixing or authorizing the use of the appraiser's signature to certify recognition and acceptance of that appraiser's USPAP responsibilities in appraisal practice. *(Bold added for emphasis.)*

The <u>Management</u> section of the ETHICS RULE requires that fees, commissions, or things of value relating to the procurement of an assignment **must be disclosed**.

> *An appraiser must disclose that he or she paid a fee or commission, or gave a thing of value in connection with the procurement of an assignment.*

The disclosure of the fee, commission, or thing of value must:

- Refer to payments being made **by the appraiser**, not to the appraiser.

- Reference to a particular assignment and not reference gifts or other things of value provided to a client as a "thank you" or other appreciation for business in general.

- Be made in the certification and in any letter of transmittal in which conclusions are stated.

- Not be required for the amount (or value) of the payment.

The <u>Management</u> section of the ETHICS RULE also states, in part:

> *An appraiser must not accept an assignment, or have a compensation arrangement for an assignment, that is contingent on any of the following:*
>
> *1. the reporting of a predetermined result (e.g., opinion of value);*
>
> ***2. a direction in assignment results that favors the cause of the client;***
>
> *3. the amount of a value opinion;*
>
> *4. the attainment of a stipulated result (e.g., that the loan closes, or taxes are reduced); or*
>
> *5. the occurrence of a subsequent event directly related to the appraiser's opinions and specific to the assignment's purpose. (USPAP 2016-2017 Edition)(Bold added for emphasis.)*

With regard to advertising, the <u>Management</u> section of the ETHICS RULE states, in part:

> *An appraiser must not advertise for or solicit assignments in a manner that is false, misleading, or exaggerated. (USPAP 2016-2017 Edition)*

The appraiser affixes his signature, or authorizes the use of his signature in an appraisal or appraisal review assignment to **certify recognition and acceptance of his obligations to USPAP**. The signature of one appraiser must not be affixed by another without the signing appraiser's consent. Authorization to affix or use an appraiser's signature can only be granted on an **assignment-by-assignment basis**.

USPAP FAQ 11

DON'T ACCEPT UNLESS YOU CAN APPRAISE FOR $XXX,000

Question: I received an appraisal request that says: "If you can't appraise the property for $XXX,000, you must not accept the appraisal assignment."

How should I respond to this appraisal request?

Response:

This request would be seen as an attempt to violate the appraiser's independence and the request itself may be illegal. Accepting such an assignment would violate the <u>Management</u> section of the ETHICS RULE, which states, in part:

An appraiser must **not** accept an assignment, or have a compensation arrangement for an assignment, that is contingent on any of the following:

1. The reporting of a predetermined result (e.g., opinion of value);

2. A direction in assignment results that favors the cause of the client;

Confidentiality Section of ETHICS RULE

Before we begin the discussion of the <u>Confidentiality</u> section of the ETHICS RULE, let's revisit the term **confidential information** from the USPAP DEFINITIONS. Confidential Information is classified as information that is either:

- *Identified by the client as confidential when providing it to an appraiser and that is not available from any other source; or*

- *Classified as confidential or private by applicable law or regulation.* (USPAP 2016-2017 Edition)

The <u>Confidentiality</u> section of the ETHICS RULE addresses, in part:

- Protection of the confidential nature of the appraiser-client relationship.

- Acting in good faith with the legitimate interests of the client relating to confidential information and in communicating assignment results.

- Obligation to be aware of and to comply with all confidentiality laws and regulations applicable in an assignment.

- Disclosure requirements and exceptions to the protection of confidential information and assignment results.

The focus of the <u>Confidentiality</u> section of the ETHICS RULE is on the appraiser-client relationship and the use of confidential information and assignment results.

> *An appraiser must not disclose (1) confidential information; or (2) assignment results to anyone other than:*

> - *The client;*

> - *Parties specifically authorized by the client;*

> - *State appraiser regulatory agencies;*

> - *Third parties as may be authorized by due process of law; or*

> - *A duly authorized professional peer review committee except when such disclosure to a committee would violate applicable law or regulation.*

√ **Note:** A member of a duly authorized professional peer review committee must not disclose confidential information presented to the committee.

3. The amount of a value opinion;

4. The attainment of a stipulated result (e.g., that the loan closes or taxes are reduced); or

5. The occurrence of a subsequent event directly related to the appraiser's opinions and specific to the assignment's purpose.

(Bold added for emphasis.)

You could respond to this request with the following statement: "I cannot accept the assignment with this condition because it violates professional ethics. You should be aware that I must develop the appraisal before I will know the results. I can only accept the assignment if you remove the predetermined value requirement."

Advisory Opinion 19, which will be discussed in Chapter 5, addresses Unacceptable Assignment Conditions in Real Property Appraisal Assignments and offers additional guidance on appraisal requests with conditions.

A <u>Comment</u> has been provided to illuminate an appraiser's options available if a redaction or process of aggregation removes all confidential elements of an assignment.

> <u>Comment</u>: *When all confidential elements of confidential information and assignment results are* **removed through redaction or the process of aggregation, client authorization is not required for the disclosure** *of the remaining information, as modified. (USPAP 2016-2017 Edition) (Bold added for emphasis)*

√ **Caution!** The appraiser has a responsibility to keep information confidential indefinitely.

USPAP FAQ 59

SAMPLE APPRAISALS AND THE ETHICS RULE

Question: I am a fee appraiser currently seeking to get on the approved list for a prospective client. In order to be considered for approval, this lender requires appraisers to provide sample appraisal reports performed within the past year.

Is there a way that I can accomplish this without violating USPAP?

Response:

In order to provide this information an appraiser must satisfy the <u>Confidentiality</u> section of the ETHICS RULE. This section states:

- An appraiser must protect the confidential nature of the appraiser-client relationship.

- An appraiser must act in good faith with regard to the legitimate interests of the client in the use of confidential information and in the communication of assignment results.

- An appraiser must be aware of, and comply with, all confidentiality and privacy laws and regulations applicable in an assignment.

- An appraiser must not disclose: (1) confidential information or (2) assignment results to anyone other than:

  1. *The client;*

  2. *Parties specifically authorized by the client;*

  3. *State appraiser regulatory agencies;*

  4. *Third parties as may be authorized by due process of law; and*

  5. *A duly authorized professional peer review committee except when such disclosure to a committee would violate applicable law or regulation.*

The <u>Comment</u> further explains that if all essential elements of confidential information are removed through redaction or the process of aggregation, client authorization is not required for the disclosure of the remaining information, as modified.

The appraiser in this case has three options:

- Decline the request to provide the information, or

- *Obtain authorization from the client of each sample appraisal report, or*

- *Provide sample reports, but redact all information that should not be provided to anyone other than the client, such as confidential information or assignment results.* (USPAP 2016-2017 Edition)

√ **Note:** Trainees should note that appraisal reports are NOT confidential to state appraiser regulatory agencies. Therefore, sample reports may be submitted to the state agency in their entirety, and without client consent, when requested by the agency.

USPAP FAQ 65

DISCLOSURE OF ASSIGNMENT RESULTS TO STATE APPRAISER REGULATORY AGENCY

Question: A new state law requires all real estate appraisers in my area to regularly submit a log to the State Appraiser Board reporting the address of properties appraised along with the value opinion.

Does this violate the confidentiality requirements in USPAP?

Response:

No. This does not violate USPAP.

The <u>Confidentiality</u> section of the ETHICS RULE states, in part:

An appraiser must not disclose: (1) confidential information or (2) assignment results to anyone other than:

- The client;
- Parties specifically authorized by the client;

State appraiser regulatory agencies; *(Bold added for emphasis.)*

- Third parties as may be authorized by due process of law; and
- A duly authorized professional peer review committee except when such disclosure to a committee would violate applicable law or regulation.

Disclosure of assignment results to the state board, or to any other entity required by law, is specifically permitted.

Overview of the RECORD KEEPING RULE

The RECORD KEEPING RULE provides numerous obligations for an appraiser regarding the appraiser's workfile, with most emphasis placed on content requirements of the workfile, and workfile custody and retention.

The Workfile

One of the specific obligations for supervisory appraisers is to **ensure compliance with workfile obligations** of USPAP. USPAP defines a **workfile** as: *Documentation necessary to support an appraiser's analyses, opinions and conclusions.* (USPAP 2016-2017 Edition)

According to the RECORD KEEPING RULE (USPAP 2016-2017 Edition):

> *An appraiser must **prepare a workfile for each appraisal or appraisal review assignment**. A workfile must be in existence prior to the issuance of any report. A written summary of an oral report must be added to the workfile within a reasonable time after the issuance of the oral report. (Bold added for emphasis)*
>
> *The workfile must include:*
>
> - *The name of the client and the identity, by name or type, of any other intended users;*
> - *True copies of all written reports, documented on any type of media. (A true copy is a replica of the report transmitted to the client. A photocopy or an electronic copy of the entire report transmitted to the client satisfies the requirement of a true copy);*
> - *Summaries of all oral reports or testimony, or a transcript of testimony, including the appraiser's signed and dated certification;*
> - *All other data, information, and documentation necessary to support the appraiser's opinions and conclusions and to show compliance with USPAP, or references to the location(s) of such other data, information, and documentation; and*
> - *A workfile in support of a Restricted Appraisal Report must be sufficient for the appraiser to produce an Appraisal Report.*

An appraiser must retain the workfile for a period of at least five years after preparation or at least two years after final disposition of any judicial proceeding in which the appraiser provided testimony related to the assignment, whichever period expires last.

An appraiser must have custody of the workfile, or make appropriate workfile retention, access, and retrieval arrangements with the party having custody of the workfile. This includes ensuring that a workfile is stored in a medium that is retrievable by the appraiser throughout the prescribed record retention period.

An appraiser having custody of a workfile must allow other appraisers with workfile obligations related to an assignment appropriate access and retrieval for the purpose of:

- *Submission to state appraiser regulatory agencies;*
- *Compliance with due process of law;*
- *Submission to a duly authorized professional peer review committee; or*
- *Compliance with retrieval arrangements.*

Comment: A workfile must be made available by the appraiser when required by a state appraiser regulatory agency or due process of law. An appraiser who willfully or knowingly fails to comply with the obligations of this RECORD KEEPING RULE is in violation of the ETHICS RULE.

USPAP FAQ 74

CONTENTS OF A WORKFILE

Question: What information must be retained in an appraiser's workfile?

Response:

An appraiser must prepare a workfile for each appraisal or appraisal review assignment. The

RECORD KEEPING RULE states:

The workfile must include:

- *The name of the client and the identity, by name or type, of any other intended users;*
- *True copies of all written reports, documented on any type of media (A true copy is a replica of the report transmitted to the client. A photocopy or an electronic copy of the entire report transmitted to the client satisfies the requirement of a true copy.);*
- *Summaries of all oral reports or testimony, or a transcript of testimony, including the appraiser's signed and dated certification;*
- *All other data, information, and documentation necessary to support the appraiser's opinions and conclusions and to show compliance with USPAP, or references to the location(s) of such other data, information, and documentation; and*
- *A workfile in support of a Restricted Appraisal Report must be sufficient for the appraiser to produce an Appraisal Report.*

The appraiser's assignment workfile serves several purposes. As in many other professions, the discipline of enforcement by public agencies and peer review, together with one's self-discipline and dedication of effort, serves to ensure performance of assignments in compliance with professional standards. In addition to facilitating enforcement, a workfile aids the appraiser in handling questions from the client or an intended user subsequent to the date of the report.

An appraiser's assignment workfile preserves evidence of the appraiser's compliance with USPAP and other information as may be required to support the appraiser's opinions and conclusions. (USPAP 2016-2017 Edition)

USPAP FAQ 81

TRAINEE ACCESS TO WORKFILES

Question: I am a trainee appraiser and have been working with the same supervising appraiser for some time. Recently, my supervising appraiser told me that since I was only a trainee, I had no right to access workfiles on appraisals where I provided significant professional assistance.

Is my supervising appraiser correct? Do trainees have no rights regarding access to workfiles?

Response:

As background, USPAP places workfile retention requirements on the appraiser. In assignments where more than one appraiser is involved (e.g., a trainee appraiser and a supervising appraiser), each appraiser shares responsibility for complying with the RECORD KEEPING RULE.

Supervising appraisers should be aware that all appraisers, including trainee appraisers, must maintain access to workfiles for a minimum of five years. A supervising appraiser must not impede a trainee appraiser's ability to access workfiles. Denying access to workfiles is a violation of the RECORD KEEPING RULE.

An appraiser having custody of a workfile must allow other appraisers with workfile obligations related to an assignment appropriate access and retrieval for the purpose of:

- Submission to state appraiser regulatory agencies;
- Compliance with due process of law;
- Submission to a duly authorized professional peer review committee; or
- Compliance with retrieval arrangements.

An appraiser who willfully or knowingly fails to comply with the obligations of this RECORD KEEPING RULE is in violation of the ETHICS RULE.

√ **Note:** See Advisory Opinion 31, Assignments Involving More than One Appraiser, for further guidance. (USPAP 2016-2017 Edition)

Overview of the COMPETENCY RULE

Competency on the part of a supervisory appraiser or trainee appraiser is likely the most critical determination that must be made in the experience process. Obviously, the trainee appraiser should be gaining competence during this period with their participation **in every assignment**. This is the purpose of the experience requirement.

Supervisory appraisers must also consider competence; not just their competence to complete a specific assignment with a trainee, but also their ability to adequately supervise a trainee. Throughout the AQB's supervisor/trainee criteria, competency, and familiarity with the COMPETENCY RULE is often referenced.

Competency in context with USPAP refers to *an appraiser's knowledge and experience to provide a service or complete an assignment.* The COMPETENCY RULE applies to appraisal practice. So, in other words, competency applies anytime one is **acting as an appraiser**, NOT only in the case of an appraisal or appraisal review assignment!

Competency could apply to the appraiser's knowledge and experience regarding:

- A specific type of property or asset.
- A market.
- A geographic area.
- An intended use.
- Specific laws and regulations.
- An analytical method.

The COMPETENCY RULE sets forth the obligations of the appraiser to have or acquire competency to adequately perform an assignment, or to decline or withdraw. Components of the COMPETENCY RULE include, in part:

- Possessing competency prior to accepting an assignment.
- Having the ability to identify the problem.
- Having knowledge and experience to competently complete the assignment.
- Recognizing and complying with pertinent laws and regulations.
- Recognizing when an appraiser lacks competency.
- Disclosing the lack of knowledge or experience before an assignment, or if facts discovered during an assignment reveal a lack of competency.
- Methods for obtaining competency if the appraiser does not already possess adequate competency.

The three sections of the COMPETENCY RULE consist of:

- **Being Competent** – Requirements for competency.
- **Acquiring Competency** – Requirements if an appraiser is not competent at the onset but wishes to accept the assignment.
- **Lack of Competency** – Requirements of an appraiser who realizes he does not possess and cannot acquire competency to complete an assignment.

Being Competent

The first section of the COMPETENCY RULE, <u>Being Competent</u>, establishes the following requirements:

- Being able to correctly identify the problem.
- Having the knowledge and experience to competently complete the assignment .
- Recognition of, and compliance with, any laws and regulations applicable to the appraiser or assignment.

In the first section, the <u>Comment</u> points out **factors the appraiser must consider when assessing his or her competency**:

> <u>Comment</u>: *Competency may apply to factors such as, but not limited to, an appraiser's familiarity with a specific type of property or asset, a market, a geographic area, an intended use, specific laws and regulations, or an analytical method. If such a factor is necessary for an appraiser to develop credible assignment results, the appraiser is responsible for having the competency to address that factor or for following the steps outlined below to satisfy this COMPETENCY RULE.*

The remainder of the revised <u>Comment</u> clarifies that the appraiser's competency applies **at the time of the assignment** when retrospective opinions and conclusions are being expressed:

> *For assignments with retrospective opinions and conclusions, the appraiser must meet the requirements of this COMPETENCY RULE at the time of the assignment, rather than the effective date. (USPAP 2016-2017 Edition)*

Acquiring Competency

The second section of the COMPETENCY RULE, **Acquiring Competency**, addresses an appraiser who lacks competency but would like to accept an assignment.

The appraiser must:

- Disclose the lack of competency to the client prior to accepting the assignment.
- Take all necessary steps to competently complete the assignment.
- Describe the lack of competency in the report, including the steps taken to competently complete the assignment.

The <u>Comment</u> to the second section of the COMPETENCY RULE addresses **how competency can be acquired.**

> *Comment: Competency can be acquired in various ways, including, but not limited to, personal study by the appraiser, association with an appraiser reasonably believed to have the necessary knowledge and/or experience, or retention of others who possess the necessary knowledge and/or experience.*

Geographic competency is but one of numerous areas where an appraiser could lack competency, however, the appraiser is still responsible for being geographically competent. This is emphasized in the remainder of the <u>Comment</u>:

> *In an assignment where geographic competency is necessary, an appraiser who is not familiar with the relevant market characteristics must acquire an understanding necessary to produce credible assignment results for the specific property type and market involved. (USPAP 2016-2017 Edition)*

Lack of Competency

The last section of the COMPETENCY RULE, <u>Lack of Competency</u>, describes the appraiser's obligation to decline or withdraw from the assignment if unable to comply with the rule to complete the assignment competently.

If during the course of an assignment, facts or conditions are discovered that cause the appraiser to realize that he or she lacks the required knowledge and experience to complete the assignment competently, the appraiser must:

- Notify the client;

- Take all necessary steps to competently complete the assignment; and

- Describe the lack of competency in the report, including the steps taken to competently complete the assignment.

USPAP FAQ 96

ACQUIRING KNOWLEDGE AND EXPERIENCE TO COMPLY WITH THE COMPETENCY RULE

Question: How does an appraiser gain the knowledge and experience required by the COMPETENCY RULE if he or she lacks the knowledge and experience to complete an assignment competently?

Response:

The COMPETENCY RULE requires an appraiser who lacks the knowledge and experience to complete an assignment competently to [a.] disclose the lack of knowledge and/or experience to the client before accepting the assignment, or [b.] disclose the lack of knowledge and/or experience to the client during the assignment if discovered by the appraiser during the assignment. In either instance, the appraiser must then take all steps necessary to appropriately complete the assignment competently and document the steps in the appraisal report. An appraiser may gain the knowledge and experience required through any or all of the following: personal study by the appraiser; association with an appraiser reasonably believed to have the necessary knowledge or experience; or, retention of others who possess the required knowledge or experience.

In addition, the COMPETENCY RULE also requires that an appraiser in an assignment must withdraw from the assignment if competency cannot be achieved prior to completion of the assignment. Refer to the COMPETENCY RULE for further guidance. (USPAP 2016-2017 Edition)

Overview of the SCOPE OF WORK RULE

Determining the appropriate scope of work in an assignment is at the core of the appraisal process. If you recall, during our discussion of the COMPETENCY RULE, in order for an appraiser to be competent, he or she must be able to properly identify the problem to be solved, which is the first step in making the scope of work decision. For trainee appraisers, participating in **problem identification** and the **scope**

of work decision are some of the first practical learning challenges that might be faced in an appraisal assignment.

Before we begin the study of the SCOPE OF WORK RULE, let's review the USPAP definition of the term scope of work:

> **Scope of Work:** *the type and extent of research and analyses in an appraisal or appraisal review assignment. (USPAP 2016-2017 Edition)*

The SCOPE OF WORK RULE addresses **three primary obligations for appraisers** in an appraisal or appraisal review assignment; each of these sections of the rule will be discussed in this lesson:

- Problem Identification
- Scope of Work Acceptability
- Disclosure Obligations

In addition, the SCOPE OF WORK RULE indicates that *for each appraisal or appraisal review assignment, an appraiser must:*

- *Identify the problem to be solved.*
- *Determine and perform the scope of work necessary to develop credible assignment results.*
- *Disclose the scope of work in the report.* (USPAP 2016-2017 Edition)

With even more functions, the SCOPE OF WORK RULE, in part:

- Establishes fundamental considerations by the appraiser in determining the proper scope of work in an assignment.
- Requires the appraiser to properly identify the problem and gather and analyze information about the assignment elements that lead the appraiser to a scope of work decision.
- Describes the role of the client in determining the scope of work in an assignment.
- Establishes a benchmark for scope of work acceptability.
- Discusses the disclosure obligations of the appraiser regarding the scope of work performed in an assignment.

In general, when an appraiser determines the appropriate scope of work to be applied in an assignment, he is making a decision regarding (but not limited to) the:

- Extent to which a property is identified.
- Extent of property inspection (tangible property).
- Type of data to be researched and to what extent.
- Type and extent of analysis applied in order to reach opinions or conclusions.

USPAP recognizes that these elements will not be the same in every assignment, or with every property. As such, the SCOPE OF WORK RULE requires that the scope of work be determined in each appraisal or appraisal review assignment.

The following excerpts, taken from the introduction of the SCOPE OF WORK RULE, are important to understand the appraiser's scope of work decision:

- *Appraisers have broad flexibility and significant responsibility in determining the appropriate scope of work for an appraisal or appraisal review assignment.*
- *The appraiser must be prepared to demonstrate that the scope of work is sufficient to produce credible assignment results.* (USPAP 2016-2017 Edition)

√ **Note:** Additional guidance about the scope of work can be found in Advisory Opinion 28 and Advisory Opinion 29.

Guidance offered by the following excerpts from Advisory Opinion 28 assist in understanding this portion of the rule:

- *USPAP recognizes that the appropriate scope of work may differ significantly for different assignments; the SCOPE OF WORK RULE provides flexibility in determining the scope of work.*
- *The competency necessary to determine an appropriate scope of work within the allowed flexibility resides with the appraiser.*
- *Therefore, while it is common and reasonable for the client to provide input to the appraiser regarding a desired scope of work, the responsibility for determining the appropriate scope of work resides with the appraiser.* (USPAP 2016-2017 Edition)

Let's review additional excerpts from the introduction of the SCOPE OF WORK RULE regarding the appraiser's scope of work decision:

- *Credible assignment results require support by relevant evidence and logic.*
- *The credibility of assignment results is always measured in the context of the intended use.*

Another term defined by USPAP is the term "credible."

Since this term is used throughout the SCOPE OF WORK RULE (and in other parts), we should review the USPAP definition of the term credible, which USPAP classifies as "*worthy of belief.*" (USPAP 2016-2017 Edition)

Problem Identification

The requirement for an appraiser to identify the problem to be solved is prominently integrated into the introduction to the SCOPE OF WORK RULE.

> *An appraiser must properly identify the problem to be solved in order to determine the appropriate scope of work.*

The obligation to identify the problem to be solved is further defined in a section of the SCOPE OF WORK RULE titled <u>Problem Identification</u>.

Overall, this section states:

- *An appraiser must gather and analyze information about those assignment elements that are necessary to properly identify the appraisal or appraisal review problem to be solved.*

The subsequent <u>Comment</u> to this section further elaborates on the elements of problem identification that must be identified.

The elements of problem identification include:

- *Clients and any other intended users;*
- *Intended use of the appraiser's opinions and conclusions;*
- *Type and definition of value;*
- *Effective date of the appraiser's opinions and conclusions;*
- *Subject of the assignment and its relevant characteristics; and*
- *Assignment conditions.*

Assignment conditions involved in problem identification include:

- Assumptions
- Extraordinary assumptions
- Hypothetical conditions
- Laws and regulations
- Jurisdictional exceptions
- Other conditions that affect the scope of work

Laws include constitutions, legislative and court-made law, administrative rules, and ordinances. Regulations include rules or orders, having legal force, issued by an administrative agency.

An example of an assignment condition applicable to supervisory appraisers and trainee appraisers might be a client-imposed prohibition that a trainee cannot inspect the subject property without the presence of their supervisory appraiser, or that a trainee cannot participate under any circumstance.

The correlation of problem identification and the appraisal process is amplified by these excerpts from Advisory Opinion 28:

- *Problem identification is the beginning point of every assignment.*

- *The appraiser must gather and analyze the information needed to properly recognize the appraisal or appraisal review problem to be solved.*

- *Identifying the problem to be solved is required in order to make critical judgments in determining the appropriate scope of work.*

- *Therefore, the assignment elements necessary for problem identification in an appraisal or appraisal review, assignment also serve as reference points in determining whether the scope of work performed was appropriate to provide credible assignment results.* (USPAP 2016-2017 Edition)

> √ **Caution!** Proper identification of the problem is necessary for compliance with the COMPETENCY RULE.

The information learned or determined by the appraiser during problem identification provides a basis for determining the type and extent of analysis to include in the development of an appraisal. Similar information is necessary for problem identification in an appraisal review assignment.

An appraiser's obligation to properly identify the problem is also found in each development Standard (1, 3, 6, 7, and 9). Identification of relevant characteristics, though, is a judgment made by the appraiser that requires competency in that type of assignment.

> √ **Note:** Scope of work addresses *only* the development process. Communication with the client is required to establish most of the information necessary for problem identification.

Acceptability

The second section of the rule, <u>Scope of Work Acceptability</u>, addresses the acceptability of the scope of work in an assignment and commences with a general obligation:

> *The scope of work must include the research and analyses that are necessary to develop credible assignment results.*

The <u>Comment</u> following this obligation defines how the appraiser determines *when* the scope of work in an assignment is acceptable.

In part, the <u>Comment</u> states:

> *The scope of work is acceptable when it meets or exceeds:*
>
> - *The expectations of parties who are regularly intended users for similar assignments;* ***and***
>
> - *What an appraiser's peers' actions would be in performing the same or a similar assignment.* (USPAP 2016-2017 Edition) (Bold added for emphasis.)

According to USPAP, **appraiser's peers** are defined as *other appraisers who have expertise and competency in a similar type of assignment.* (USPAP 2016-2017 Edition)

The Comment continues:

- *Determining the scope of work in an assignment is an ongoing process throughout the assignment.*

An appraiser may reconsider or change the scope of work during the course of an assignment, based on information or conditions that the appraiser discovers.

√ **Note:** If any investigation, information, method, or technique would appear relevant to the client, another intended user, or the appraiser's peers, an appraiser must be prepared to support the decision for its exclusion.

Let's look again at Advisory Opinion 28, which has additional guidance for an appraiser in deciding the scope of work through these excerpts:

- *Determining the appropriate scope of work requires judgment.*
- *This judgment rests on the appraiser's identification of the assignment elements and understanding of what is required to solve the identified problem.*
- *In many assignments, experienced appraisers are able to make this judgment about the appropriate scope of work quickly because they have performed many assignments addressing a similar problem to be solved (assignment with similar assignment elements).*
- *In other assignments, the determination of the appropriate scope of work may require more analysis by the appraiser because the problem to be solved has certain unusual characteristics. In yet other assignments, the appraiser may begin with a planned scope of work but in the course of the assignment find that the planned scope of work must be modified in order to produce credible assignment results. (USPAP 2016-2017 Edition)*

Advisory Opinion 29 is specifically focused on guidance regarding the acceptability of the scope of work. In this excerpt from Advisory Opinion 29, the discussion of an "appraiser's peers" is helpful:

To be an appraiser's peer for a particular assignment, one must have the competency to address the appraisal problem presented in that assignment. This includes the knowledge and experience to:

- *Properly identify the appraisal or appraisal review problem to be solved;*
- *Determine the type and extent of research and analyses to include in the development process; and*
- *Perform the required research and analyses properly. (USPAP 2016-2017 Edition)*

Advisory Opinion 29 further advises:

- *Because assignments can require different types of expertise and competency, it is possible to be considered an appraiser's peer for some assignments, but not for others.*
- *Identifying an appraiser's peer is always done in the context of a particular assignment.*
- *An appraiser can have a focused area of expertise and competency or a wide variety of expertise and competency.*
- *Merely holding the same type or level of credential does not make one an appraiser's peer.*
- *Determining if an individual is an appraiser's peer requires examining the individual's expertise regarding each of the elements that define the assignment.*

  For example, solely having expertise in appraising the same type of property is not sufficient to make someone an appraiser's peer. (USPAP 2016-2017 Edition)

The Scope of Work Acceptability section continues with a specific prohibition regarding the scope of work:

An appraiser must not allow assignment conditions to limit the scope of work to such a degree that the assignment results are not credible in the context of the intended use. (USPAP 2016-2017 Edition)

The <u>Comment</u> following this prohibition provides further guidance as to how the appraiser must proceed in such circumstances:

If relevant information is not available because of assignment conditions that limit research opportunities (such as conditions that place limitations on inspection or information gathering), an appraiser must withdraw from the assignment unless the appraiser can:

- *Modify the assignment conditions to expand the scope of work to include gathering the information; or*

- *Use an extraordinary assumption about such information, if credible assignment results can still be developed.*

A final obligation in the <u>Scope of Work Acceptability</u> section contains another specific prohibition regarding bias:

An appraiser must not allow the intended use of an assignment or a client's objectives to cause the assignment results to be biased.

Disclosure Obligations

The scope of work that was performed in an assignment must be disclosed in the report.

The final section of the SCOPE OF WORK RULE, <u>Disclosure Obligations</u>, presents a general disclosure obligation for the scope of work, plus a <u>Comment</u> that contains the rationale for the obligation and explanation of "sufficient information."

The report must contain sufficient information to allow intended users to understand the scope of work performed.

<u>Comment</u>: Proper disclosure is required because clients and other intended users rely on the assignment results. Sufficient information includes disclosure of research and analyses performed and might also include disclosure of research and analyses not performed. (USPAP 2016-2017 Edition)

Here, we once more look to Advisory Opinion 28 for additional guidance regarding disclosure of the scope of work through these excerpts:

- *An appraiser must disclose research and analyses not performed when such disclosure is necessary for intended users to understand the report properly and not be misled.*

- *These disclosure requirements apply to the scope of work performed, rather than the scope of work initially planned by the appraiser.*

- *The appraiser must disclose the type and extent of research and analyses that were actually completed in the development process.*

- *Additionally, the information required to allow intended users to understand the scope of work may include disclosure of research and analyses not performed.*

- *There is no requirement for the scope of work description to be in a particular or separate section of the report. (USPAP 2016-2017 Edition)*

USPAP FAQ 159

JUDGING THE ACTIONS OF AN APPRAISER'S PEERS

Question: In the SCOPE OF WORK RULE, one of the two tests regarding the acceptability of an appraiser's scope of work is what the appraiser's peers would do.

There are many appraisers that do things differently, so how would I know what they would do in an assignment?

Response:

The SCOPE OF WORK RULE states that the acceptability of an appraiser's work is judged based on two tests:

- *The expectations of parties who are regularly intended users for similar assignments; and*
- *What an appraiser's peers' actions would be in performing the same or a similar assignment.*

*The first step in knowing what your peers would do is to identify your peers. In USPAP, the term **appraiser's peers** has a specific meaning. It is defined as:*

- Other appraisers who have expertise and competency in a similar type of assignment.

This definition illustrates that an appraiser's peers are assignment specific and may change from assignment to assignment. This is because appraisers have varying levels of expertise and competency in specific property types, geographic locations, or other important areas of appraisal.

√ **Note:** For more information on appraiser's peers, please see Advisory Opinion 29, An Acceptable Scope of Work.

Knowledge about what an appraiser's peers would do in a similar assignment comes through being a participant in the profession. Typical forums that allow appraisal professionals to share information about practice include appraisal journals and publications, professional meetings and conferences, education though courses and seminars, and appraisal discussion groups. (USPAP 2016-2017 Edition)

USPAP FAQ 175

DOES INSPECTION OF SUBJECT PROPERTY MEAN A PHYSICAL INSPECTION?

Question: I am a licensed trainee with approximately six months of experience. My supervisory appraiser recently determined that I am competent to perform inspections on my own; however, many of our clients require the supervisory appraiser to physically inspect the property as well.

If I do the inspection by myself, but take numerous representative photos of the interior of the subject property, may my supervisory appraiser indicate in the report that he also inspected the property?

Response:

No. A physical inspection of the interior of the property is not the same as a physical inspection of photographs of the interior of the property. It would be misleading for any appraiser, including supervisory appraisers, to indicate that a physical inspection was performed when, in fact, the appraiser viewed photographs of the property. An appraiser who only inspects photographs of a property, but signs a certification indicating that he or she physically inspected the subject property, is in violation of the USPAP prohibition against communicating assignment results with the intent to mislead or to defraud, communicating a report that is known by the appraiser to be misleading or fraudulent, and, possibly, knowingly permitting an employee or other person to communicate a misleading or fraudulent report. (See Conduct section of the ETHICS RULE.) (USPAP 2016-2017 Edition)

Chapter Summary

1. The ETHICS RULE sets forth foundational obligations when acting in the role of an appraiser and amplifies that an appraiser is required to always observe the highest standards of professional ethics.

2. Protected classes or related characteristics of those classes that are indicated in USPAP include race, color, religion, national origin, gender, marital status, familial status, age, receipt of public assistance income, and handicap.

3. Any services as an appraiser, or in any other capacity, regarding the subject property performed within a three-year period prior to acceptance of the assignment must be disclosed to the client.

4. The Management section of the ETHICS RULE addresses, in part, disclosing fees, commissions, or things of value paid in connection with the procurement of an assignment, unacceptable assignment conditions and compensation arrangements, advertising/soliciting assignments in a false, misleading, or exaggerated manner, and affixing or authorizing the use of the appraiser's signature to certify recognition and acceptance of that appraiser's USPAP responsibilities in appraisal practice.

5. The focus of the Confidentiality section of the ETHICS RULE is on the appraiser-client relationship and the use of confidential information and assignment results.

6. The RECORD KEEPING RULE provides numerous obligations for an appraiser regarding the appraiser's workfile, with most emphasis placed on content requirements of the workfile, and workfile custody and retention.

7. The three sections of the COMPETENCY RULE consist of (1) Being Competent – Requirements for competency, (2) Acquiring Competency – Requirements if an appraiser is not competent at the onset but wishes to accept the assignment, (3) Lack of Competency – Requirements of an appraiser who realizes he does not possess and cannot acquire competency to complete an assignment.

8. Competency on the part of a supervisory appraiser or trainee appraiser is one of the most critical determination that must be made in the experience process.

9. The SCOPE OF WORK RULE addresses three primary obligations for appraisers in an appraisal or appraisal review assignment: (1) Problem Identification, (2) Scope of Work Acceptability, and (3) Disclosure Obligations

Chapter Quiz

1. *Brad is acting as a supervisory appraiser for Tina, a trainee appraiser. Brad has told Tina that he keeps all of his workfiles for at least ten years, although, according to the RECORD KEEPING RULE, a workfile must be kept for a minimum of _____ years.*

   A. three
   B. four
   C. five
   D. seven

2. *Trainee appraiser Sarah is concerned that the scope of work she determined in an assignment may not be sufficient. According to the SCOPE OF WORK RULE, credibility of assignment results is always measured in context of the*

   A. client's goals.
   B. highest and best use.
   C. intended use.
   D. intended user.

3. *Jason's supervisory appraiser is discussing the ETHICS RULE of USPAP with him and reviewing the prohibitions included in the rule. Which of these activities does the Conduct section of the ETHICS RULE prohibit?*

   A. engaging in criminal conduct
   B. objective opinions in appraisal practice
   C. performing in another professional role
   D. valuation services outside of appraisal practice

4. *A supervisory appraiser is reviewing the elements of problem identification with her trainee in order to determine the scope of work in an assignment. Which is NOT a specific element of problem identification used in determining the scope of work?*

   A. assignment conditions
   B. client and other intended users
   C. effective date of the opinions and conclusions
   D. reporting option to be used in the assignment

5. *Michael is a supervisory appraiser who has extensive experience in numerous areas of appraisal practice. However, there are certain valuation techniques and types of properties for which Michael has had no experience. Which would NOT be considered a competency factor in a particular assignment?*

   A. analytical method
   B. appraiser's credentials
   C. intended use
   D. laws and regulations

6. *Stephen, a supervisory appraiser, has accepted an appraisal review assignment, which he will also share with his trainee, Sandy. The assignment includes an oral report as the only means of communication. When must Stephen and Sandy initiate a workfile for an oral report?*

   A. at the time of issuing the report
   B. before accepting an assignment
   C. prior to the issuance of the report
   D. within a reasonable period of time after the report

7. *The Management section of the ETHICS RULE states that an appraiser must disclose that he or she paid a fee or commission, or gave a thing of value in connection with the procurement of an assignment by including the disclosure in the*

   A. certification only.
   B. workfile only.
   C. certification and transmittal letters.
   D. workfile and report conclusion section.

8. *According to the Acquiring Competency section of the COMPETENCY RULE, an appraiser who lacks competency*

   A. may accept the assignment and does not need to disclose the lack of competency as long as the appraiser has taken steps to competently complete the assignment.
   B. may accept the assignment, as long as the lack of competency is disclosed to the client.
   C. may accept an assignment, as long as the lack of competency is documented in the report along with the steps taken to complete the assignment competently.
   D. may not accept the assignment.

9. *Advisory Opinion 29 states that*

   A. an appraiser's peer must have a focused area of expertise and competency specific to the designation.
   B. an appraiser's peer must have a wide variety of expertise and competency to be designated.
   C. merely holding the same type or level of credential does not make one an appraiser's peer.
   D. the type or level of credential is the sole deciding factor in the identification of an appraiser's peer.

Chapter 4

Supervisors, Trainees, and Standards Rules

Now that the RECORD KEEPING, SCOPE OF WORK, COMPETENCY, and ETHICS RULES have been outlined, we will turn our focus to specific standards rules of appraisal practice. Specifically, our discussion will be concentrated upon selected Standards Rules for developing and communicating a real property appraisal to enhance the supervisory and trainee appraiser relationship for appraisers. Ensuring trainee compliance with these Standards Rules—and USPAP in its entirety—is an important aspect of the supervisor's responsibility towards training a competent appraiser.

An overview of Advisory Opinion 31 will also be presented and evaluated. Again, relevant USPAP Frequently Asked Questions (FAQ) and USPAP Advisory Opinions will be illustrated to further explore possible nuances of the Standards Rules.

Key Terms

Report Written or oral communication that is transmitted to the client by an appraiser upon completion of an assignment.

Chapter Objectives

After completing this chapter, you will be able to:

- Describe certain Standards Rules of USPAP and how they relate to supervisory appraisers and trainee appraisers.

- Define Advisory Opinion 31 and how it relates to supervisory appraisers and trainee appraisers.

Overview of STANDARD 1

STANDARD 1 establishes a benchmark of criteria for measuring ethics and competency in the development process and contains **six Standards Rules** (**1-1** through **1-6**) that identify applicable requirements and guidance for developing an appraisal of real property.

STANDARD 1, in addition to reciting general obligations, contains requirements that can be considered a checklist correlating with the development steps in the appraisal process (Steps 1-5), from identifying the problem to be solved through reconciliation.

The introduction to STANDARD 1 provides an overview of an appraiser's general obligations:

> *In developing a real property appraisal, an appraiser must identify the problem to be solved, determine the scope of work necessary to solve the problem, and correctly complete research and analyses necessary to produce a credible appraisal.*
>
> *Comment: STANDARD 1 is directed toward the substantive aspects of developing a credible appraisal of real property. The requirements set forth in STANDARD 1 follow the appraisal development process in the order of topics addressed and can be used by appraisers and the users of appraisal services as a convenient checklist.* (USPAP 2016-2017 Edition)

Standards Rule 1-1 elaborates on requirements found in the COMPETENCY RULE and places obligation on the appraiser to:

- Be aware of, understand, and correctly employ recognized methods and techniques necessary to produce credible results.

- Not commit a substantial error of omission or commission that significantly affects an appraisal.

- Not render appraisal services in a careless or negligent manner.

Standards Rule 1-1(a): Methods and Techniques

Standards Rule 1-1(a) addresses the obligation of the appraiser to keep current with methods and techniques:

> *In developing a real property appraisal, an appraiser must:*
>
> *(a) be aware of, understand, and correctly employ those recognized methods and techniques that are necessary to produce a credible appraisal.* (USPAP 2016-2017 Edition)

The <u>Comment</u> to this portion of this Standards Rule reminds appraisers that changes and developments in the real estate industry have a significant impact on the appraisal profession. Appraisers have an obligation to keep abreast with changes in the cost and manner of construction as well as marketing commercial, industrial, and residential real estate.

 Caution! Appraisers need to realize that changes occurring in the legal framework in which real property rights and interests are created, conveyed, and mortgaged have resulted in corresponding changes in appraisal theory.

Social changes have also affected appraisal theory and practice. The appraisal profession is constantly revisiting and revising appraisal methods and techniques, as well as developing new methods and techniques to meet new circumstances.

 Caution! It is not sufficient for appraisers to simply maintain the skills and the knowledge they initially possessed. Each appraiser must continuously improve his or her skills to remain proficient in real property appraisal.

USPAP and the Appraisal Process

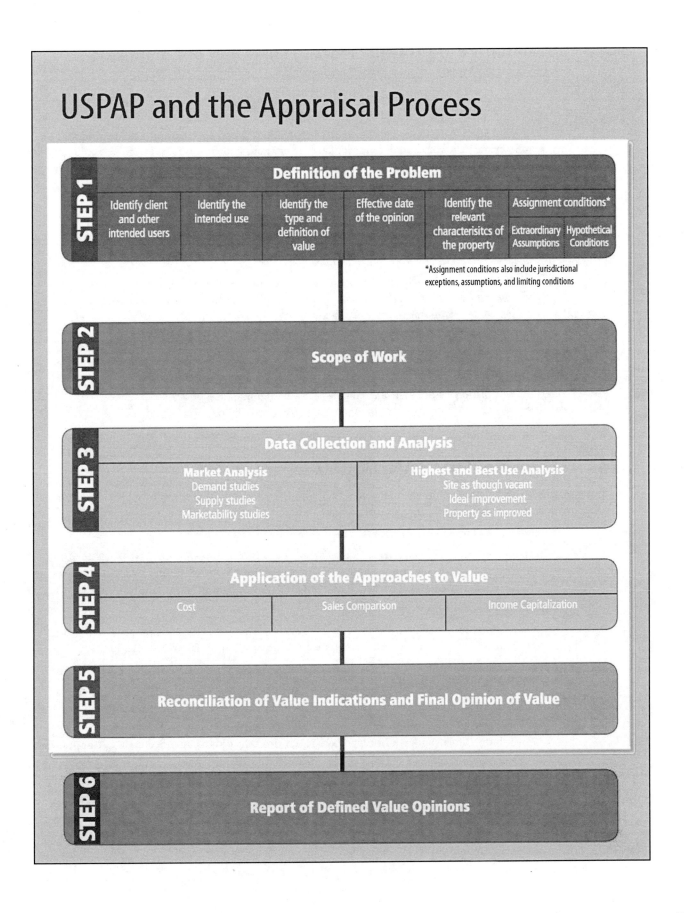

STEP 1

Definition of the Problem

Identify client and other intended users	Identify the intended use	Identify the type and definition of value	Effective date of the opinion	Identify the relevant characterisitcs of the property	Assignment conditions*	
					Extraordinary Assumptions	Hypothetical Conditions

*Assignment conditions also include jurisdictional exceptions, assumptions, and limiting conditions

STEP 2

Scope of Work

STEP 3

Data Collection and Analysis

Market Analysis Demand studies Supply studies Marketability studies	**Highest and Best Use Analysis** Site as though vacant Ideal improvement Property as improved

STEP 4

Application of the Approaches to Value

Cost	Sales Comparison	Income Capitalization

STEP 5

Reconciliation of Value Indications and Final Opinion of Value

STEP 6

Report of Defined Value Opinions

Standards Rule 1-1(b): Errors of Omission or Commission

Standards Rule 1-1(b) describes the obligation for an appraiser to not commit errors:

- *In developing a real property appraisal, an appraiser must not commit a substantial error of omission or commission that significantly affects an appraisal.*

The <u>Comment</u> to this phrase of the Standards Rule reminds appraisers that they must use sufficient care to avoid errors that would significantly affect their opinions and conclusions. Diligence is required to identify and analyze the factors, conditions, data, and other information that would have a significant effect on the credibility of the assignment results.

Standards Rule 1-1(c): Carelessness and Negligence

Standards Rule 1-1(c) describes the obligation for an appraiser to not be careless or negligent:

In developing a real property appraisal, an appraiser must:

- *Not render appraisal services in a careless or negligent manner, such as by making a series of errors that, although individually might not significantly affect the results of an appraisal, in the aggregate affects the credibility of those results.*

The <u>Comment</u> to this obligation of the Standards Rule recognizes that perfection is impossible to attain, and competence does not require perfection.

√ *Caution!* Appraisers are warned to not render appraisal services in a careless or negligent manner and to use due diligence and due care.

Overview of STANDARD 2

STANDARD 2 addresses the obligations of an appraiser for **reporting a real property appraisal** and correlates with **Step 6** in the appraisal process.

See *USPAP and the Appraisal Process Flowchart – Step 6, at right.*

The term "**report**" refers to *written or oral communication that is transmitted to the client by an appraiser upon completion of an assignment.* STANDARD 2 contains **four Standards Rules** (**2-1** through **2-4**).

The Introduction to STANDARD 2 reinforces the appraiser's obligation to not report a real property appraisal in a manner that is misleading:

In reporting the results of a real property appraisal, an appraiser must communicate each analysis, opinion, and conclusion in a manner that is not misleading. (USPAP 2016-2017 Edition)

The <u>Comment</u> accompanying the Introduction contains general clarifications regarding STANDARD 2 and real property appraisal reporting:

- The standard addresses the **content and level of information** required in a report and does not dictate the form, format, or style of the report.

- The form, format, and style of a report are **specific to the needs of intended users and appraisers**.

- The substantive content of a report determines **compliance with the reporting options** permitted by STANDARD 2.

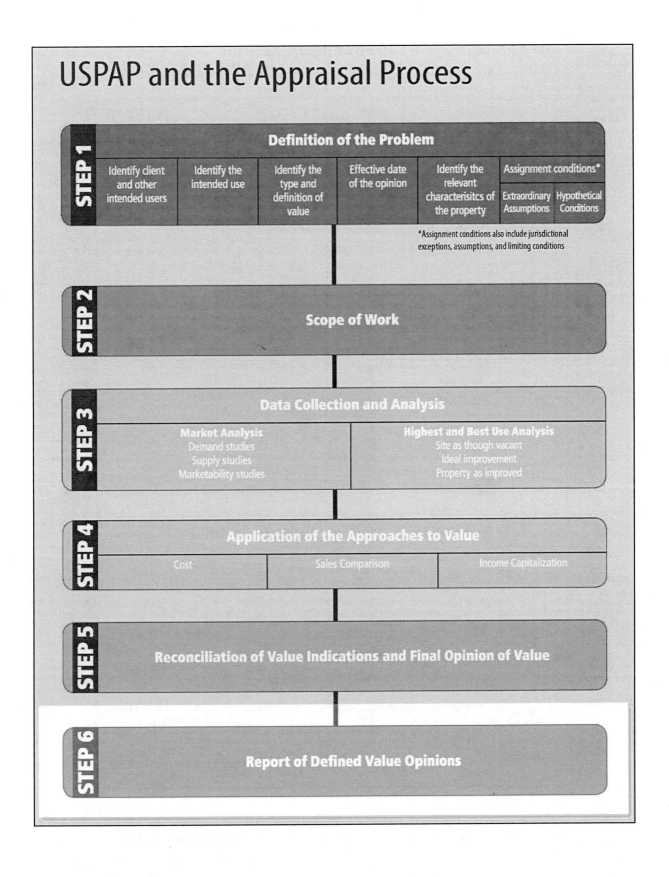

USPAP and the Appraisal Process

STEP 1

Definition of the Problem

Identify client and other intended users	Identify the intended use	Identify the type and definition of value	Effective date of the opinion	Identify the relevant characterisitcs of the property	Assignment conditions*	
					Extraordinary Assumptions	Hypothetical Conditions

*Assignment conditions also include jurisdictional exceptions, assumptions, and limiting conditions

STEP 2

Scope of Work

STEP 3

Data Collection and Analysis

Market Analysis	Highest and Best Use Analysis
Demand studies	Site as though vacant
Supply studies	Ideal improvement
Marketability studies	Property as improved

STEP 4

Application of the Approaches to Value

Cost	Sales Comparison	Income Capitalization

STEP 5

Reconciliation of Value Indications and Final Opinion of Value

STEP 6

Report of Defined Value Opinions

Standards Rule 2-1: General Obligations

Standards Rule 2-1 contains **general obligations** for all written and oral real property appraisal reports:

Each written or oral real property appraisal report must:

(a) clearly and accurately set forth the appraisal in a manner that will not be misleading;

(b) contain sufficient information to enable the intended users of the appraisal to understand the report properly; and

(c) clearly and accurately disclose all assumptions, extraordinary assumptions, hypothetical conditions, and limiting conditions used in the assignment.

Standards Rule 2-3: Signed Certification

Under Standards Rule 2-3 (USPAP 2016-2017 Edition), all written real property appraisal reports (for **both** reporting options) must contain a signed certification containing language similar to the following:

I certify that, to the best of my knowledge and belief:

- *The statements of fact contained in this report are true and correct.*

- *The reported analyses, opinions, and conclusions are limited only by the reported assumptions and limiting conditions and are my personal, impartial, and unbiased professional analyses, opinions, and conclusions.*

- *I have no (or the specified) present or prospective interest in the property that is the subject of this report and no (or the specified) personal interest with respect to the parties involved.*

- *I have performed no (or the specified) services, as an appraiser or in any other capacity, regarding the property that is the subject of this report within the three-year period immediately preceding acceptance of this assignment.*

- *I have no bias with respect to the property that is the subject of this report or to the parties involved with this assignment.*

- *My engagement in this assignment was not contingent upon developing or reporting predetermined results.*

- *My compensation for completing this assignment is not contingent upon the development or reporting of a predetermined value or direction in value that favors the cause of the client, the amount of the value opinion, the attainment of a stipulated result, or the occurrence of a subsequent event directly related to the intended use of this appraisal.*

- *My analyses, opinions, and conclusions were developed, and this report has been prepared, in conformity with the Uniform Standards of Professional Appraisal Practice.*

- *I have (or have not) made a personal inspection of the property that is the subject of this report. (If more than one person signs this certification, the certification must clearly specify which individuals did and which individuals did not make a personal inspection of the appraised property.)*

- *No one provided significant real property appraisal assistance to the person signing this certification. (If there are exceptions, the name of each individual providing significant real property appraisal assistance must be stated.)*

The Comment to Standards Rule 2-3 is fairly extensive and, in some cases, covers a variety of appraisal scenarios. It states, in part:

- *A signed certification is an integral part of the appraisal report. An appraiser who signs any part of the appraisal report, including a letter of transmittal must also sign the certification.*

In an assignment that includes only assignment results developed by the real property appraiser(s), any appraiser(s) who signs a certification accepts full responsibility for all elements of the certification, for the assignment results, and for the contents of the appraisal report.

DOES USPAP DEFINE SUPERVISORY APPRAISER?

Question: The term supervisory appraiser is used in many appraisal reports, particularly residential appraisal reports.

Does USPAP define supervisory appraiser?

Response:

No. USPAP does not define or otherwise address this term. The term supervisory appraiser was introduced by the authors of several widely used residential appraisal report forms. However, it should be noted that an appraiser who signs any part of the appraisal report, including a letter of transmittal, must also sign the certification. (USPAP 2016-2017 Edition)

DISAGREE WITH SUPERVISOR ON VALUE CONCLUSION

Question: I am employed at a firm where my reports are reviewed by a supervisory appraiser. The supervisory appraiser recently asked me to make changes to a report that resulted in a value opinion with which I do not agree. I am not comfortable signing the amended report.

What are my obligations under USPAP?

Response:

If the report does not represent your own opinions and conclusions, then you must not sign the report or the certification.

The <u>Comment</u> to Standards Rule 2-3 states: An appraiser who signs any part of an appraisal report, including a letter of transmittal, must also sign a certification... which must include a statement similar to:

- *I certify that, to the best of my knowledge and belief, the reported analyses, opinions, and conclusions are limited only by the reported assumptions and limiting conditions and are my **personal**, impartial, and unbiased professional analyses, opinions, and conclusions. (Bold added for emphasis)*

An appraiser required to make changes that he or she does not agree with would not be reporting his or her own personal analyses, opinions, or conclusions. (USPAP 2016-2017 Edition)

Standards Rule 2-3: Non-Real Property Assets and Work Done by Others

The next portion of the <u>Comment</u> applies when the assignment additionally includes opinions or conclusions related to **non-real property assets**.

> *...In an assignment that includes personal property, business or intangible asset assignment results not developed by the real property appraiser(s), any real property appraiser(s) who signs a certification accepts full responsibility for the real property elements of the certification, for the real property assignment results, and for the real property contents of the appraisal report.*

Clarification is provided within the <u>Comment</u> that when an assignment includes non-real property assets; the **real** property appraiser signing the certification is taking full responsibility only for the **real** property related elements.

The <u>Comment</u> to Standards Rule 2-3 continues with obligations of a real property appraiser when he has relied on **work done by others who do not sign the certification**. An example of such case might be (but not limited to) when a real property appraiser has relied on the opinions and conclusions of non-real property appraisers when their opinions and conclusions are incorporated into the real property appraiser's opinions and conclusions.

> *When a signing appraiser(s) has relied on work done by appraisers and others who do not sign the certification, the signing appraiser is responsible for the decision to rely on their work. The signing appraiser(s) is required to have a reasonable basis for believing that those individuals performing the*

work are competent. The signing appraiser(s) also must have no reason to doubt that the work of those individuals is credible. (USPAP 2016-2017 Edition)

Standards Rule 2-3: Other Appraisal Assistance

The remainder of the <u>Comment</u> addresses disclosure in circumstances when **other individuals provide significant appraisal assistance** to the real property appraisers who are not signing the certification.

The names of individuals providing significant real property appraisal assistance who do not sign a certification must be stated in the certification. It is not required that the description of their assistance be contained in the certification, **but disclosure of their assistance is required in accordance with Standards Rule 2-2 (a)(vii) or (b)(vii),** *as applicable.* (Bold added for emphasis)

Regarding appraisal assistance for an appraisal report, the <u>Comment</u> for Standards Rule 2-2(a)(vii) (Appraisal Report) states:

When any portion of the work involves significant real property appraisal assistance, the appraiser must **summarize** *the extent of that assistance. The name(s) of those providing the significant real property appraisal assistance must be stated in the certification, in accordance with Standards Rule 2-3.* (USPAP 2016-2017 Edition) (Bold added for emphasis)

Regarding appraisal assistance for a restricted appraisal report, the <u>Comment</u> for Standards Rule 2-2(b)(vii) (Restricted Appraisal Report) states:

When any portion of the work involves significant real property appraisal assistance, the appraiser must **state** *the extent of that assistance. The name(s) of those providing the significant real property appraisal assistance must be stated in the certification, in accordance with Standards Rule 2-3.* (USPAP 2016-2017 Edition) (Bold added for emphasis)

USPAP FAQ 248

SIGNIFICANT APPRAISAL ASSISTANCE

Question: In preparing an appraisal assignment, I talk with many different people. I know the report certification must identify individuals who provide significant real property appraisal assistance.

What is significant appraisal assistance?

Response:

USPAP does not include a definition of significant appraisal assistance. However, aspects of this phrase can be explored to clarify its meaning.

First, the adjective significant means that the contribution must be of substance to the development of the assignment results. In other words, the individual must contribute to the valuation analysis in a noteworthy way. An individual who merely collects or provides data for use in the analysis does not provide significant appraisal assistance.

Secondly, the reference to the term appraisal assistance means that the contribution is related to the appraisal process or requires appraiser competency. One misconception is that non-appraisers who provide assistance should be identified in the certification. This is incorrect because the certification requirements in USPAP apply only to appraisers. Thus, only appraisers sign the certification or are identified as providing significant appraisal assistance.

For example, the use of an environmental expert to determine wetland boundaries would not be considered significant real property appraisal assistance.

Examples of contributions made by appraisers that constitute significant real property appraisal assistance include the identification of comparable properties and data, inspection of the subject property and comparables, estimating accrued depreciation, or forecasting income and expenses.
(USPAP 2016-2017 Edition)

USPAP FAQ 253

REPORTING SIGNIFICANT REAL PROPERTY APPRAISAL ASSISTANCE

Question: I am currently working in an appraisal firm as a trainee. As part of my training, I contribute significant real property appraisal assistance in appraisal assignments performed by other appraisers in the firm, but I do not sign the appraisal report or the certification. I understand that my name must be stated in the certification.

Must the certification include a description of my assistance?

Response:

No. A description of your assistance or contribution to the assignment is not required in the certification. However, in accordance with Standards Rule 2-2(a)(vii) and (b)(vii) the extent of the assistance must be summarized or stated (depending on the reporting option used) within the report. This required disclosure could be included within the certification, but it could also be included in some other section of the report.

√ **Note:** See AO-31: Assignments Involving More than One Appraiser, for further guidance. (USPAP 2016-2017 Edition)

Standards Rule 3-6

Standards Rule 3-6 (USPAP 2016-2017 Edition) presents the **certification requirements** for an **Appraisal Review Report**, which is similar to the certification requirements found in STANDARD 2 (*minor differences are in BOLD for emphasis*):

Each written Appraisal Review Report must contain a signed certification that is similar in content to the form located on the following screen.

I certify that, to the best of my knowledge and belief:

- *The statements of fact contained in this report are true and correct.*

- *The reported analyses, opinions, and conclusions are limited only by the reported assumptions and limiting conditions and are my personal, impartial, and unbiased professional analyses, opinions, and conclusions.*

- *I have no (or the specified) present or prospective interest in the property that is the subject of **the work under review** and no (or the specified) personal interest with respect to the parties involved.*

- *I have performed no (or the specified) other services, as an appraiser or in any other capacity, regarding the property that is the subject **of the work under review** within the three-year period immediately preceding acceptance of this assignment.*

- *I have no bias with respect to the property that is the subject **of the work under review** or to the parties involved with this assignment.*

- *My engagement in this assignment was not contingent upon developing or reporting predetermined results.*

- *My compensation is not contingent on an action or event resulting from the analyses, opinions, or conclusions in this **review** or from its use.*

- *My compensation for completing this assignment is not contingent upon the development or reporting of predetermined assignment results or assignment results that favors the cause of the client, the attainment of a stipulated result, or the occurrence of a subsequent event directly related to the intended use of this appraisal review.*

- *My analyses, opinions, and conclusions were developed and this **review report** was prepared in conformity with the Uniform Standards of Professional Appraisal Practice.*

- *I have (or have not) made a personal inspection of the subject of **the work under review**. (If more than one person signs this certification, the certification must clearly specify which individuals did and which individuals did not make a personal inspection of the **subject of the work under review**.) (For **reviews** of a business or intangible asset appraisal assignment, the inspection portion of the certification is not applicable.)*

- *No one provided significant appraisal or **appraisal review assistance** to the person signing this certification. (If there are exceptions, the name of each individual(s) providing appraisal or appraisal review assistance must be stated.)*

Cosigning a Report vs. an Appraisal Review

The <u>Comment</u> to Standards Rule 3-6 is very similar to that found in Standards Rule 2-3, with the exception that the <u>Comment</u> to Standards Rule 3-6 specifically warns that **appraisal review is a completely different activity than cosigning a report**, such as when a supervisory appraiser cosigns with a trainee.

> <u>Comment</u>: *A signed certification is an integral part of the **Appraisal Review Report**. A **reviewer** who signs any part of the **appraisal review report**, including a letter of transmittal, must also sign the certification.*
>
> *Any **reviewer** who signs a certification accepts responsibility for all elements of the certification, for the assignment results, and for the contents of the **Appraisal Review Report**.*
>
> ***Appraisal review is distinctly different from the cosigning activity addressed in Standards Rules 2-3, 6-9, 8-3, and 10-3. To avoid confusion between these activities, a reviewer performing an appraisal review must not sign the work under review unless he or she intends to accept responsibility as a cosigner of that work.***
>
> *When a signing appraiser has relied on work done by appraisers and others who do not sign the certification, the signing appraiser is responsible for the decision to rely on their work. The signing appraiser is required to have a reasonable basis for believing that those individuals performing the work are competent. The signing appraiser also must have no reason to doubt that the work of those individuals is credible.*
>
> *The names of individuals providing significant appraisal **or appraisal review assistance** who do not sign a certification must be stated in the certification. It is not required that the description of their assistance be contained in the certification, but disclosure of their assistance is required in accordance with Standards Rule 3-5(g).*

The <u>Comment</u> to Standards Rule 3-5 (g) states (in part):

- *When any portion of the work involves significant appraisal or appraisal review assistance, the reviewer must **state the extent of that assistance**. The signing reviewer must also state the name(s) of those providing the significant assistance in the certification, in accordance with Standards Rule 3-6.*

√ **Caution!** Fannie Mae and some other intended users do not permit a reviewer to have significant assistance in an assignment. Therefore, a trainee **cannot** participate in such an assignment.

Advisory Opinion 31: More than One Appraiser

Advisory Opinion 31 (AO-31) provides further insight into circumstances when there is **more than one appraiser** involved in an assignment. This Advisory Opinion applies to **real property, personal property, and intangible property**.

THE ISSUE:

What are the specific USPAP obligations when an appraisal or appraisal review assignment involves more than one appraiser? (USPAP Advisory Opinions 2016-2017 Edition)

AO-31 addresses the issue with clarification and guidance in the form of:

- Relevant USPAP References
- Record Keeping Requirements
- Certifications/Signatures
- Illustrations

When assignments involve more than one appraiser, there are often questions about the proper way to deal with USPAP requirements relating to record keeping, signatures and certifications.

It is important to realize that USPAP does not define an "appraiser" in terms of state licensing or certification requirements. USPAP defines an appraiser as one who is expected to perform valuation services competently and in a manner that is independent, impartial, and objective.

Expectation is the crucial element in determining when one is acting as an appraiser. As a result, one could be a trainee by state licensing requirements and also identified as an appraiser by USPAP definition. Reference to applicable state law should be made to clarify the specific definition of appraiser and trainee in a jurisdiction.

When an assignment is performed by more than one appraiser, each appraiser is subject to the same obligations regarding the workfile for the assignment, whether or not the appraiser signs the certification. These obligations may be met by creating a copy of the workfile for every appraiser involved in the assignment. Alternatively, the appraisers might agree in writing to an access arrangement whereby the workfile is stored in a single location but access is provided to all appraisers involved. In whatever manner this USPAP requirement is met, all appraisers involved with the assignment must meet it. (USPAP Advisory Opinions 2016-2017 Edition)

To round out your understanding of Advisory Opinion 31 within this chapter, AO-31 provides six scenarios and illustrations to help explore certain situations outlined in USPAP Advisory Opinions. A situation will be introduced and then an Advisory Opinion response will be provided following the scenario.

Illustration 1

Advisory Opinion 31 – Illustration 1 *Workfile Obligations When Trainee Signs the Report*
(USPAP Advisory Opinions 2016-2017 Edition)

Jennifer is currently being trained as an appraiser (a trainee) working toward her state license as a real property appraiser. Her work includes completing and co-signing appraisal reports with her supervising appraiser. Must she keep a copy of the workfile for every assignment she works on?

If Jennifer acted as an appraiser in the assignment, USPAP provides two options: 1) she can maintain custody of the workfile, either the original or a copy; or 2) she can make appropriate access arrangements for the retention period, for example, with her employer or supervising appraiser.

Some common scenarios in such an assignment may include the trainee appraiser and the supervising appraiser each keeping a copy of the workfile. Or, the supervising appraiser may retain custody of the workfile and provide for access by the trainee appraiser.

√ **Note:** Both of these arrangements meet the record keeping requirements.

Illustration 2

Advisory Opinion 31 – Illustration 2

Certification Requirements When Trainee Does Not Sign the Report

(USPAP Advisory Opinions 2016-2017 Edition)

Using the same scenario from Illustration 1 except only the senior appraiser signs the report and not the trainee appraiser, what certification requirements must each appraiser meet to comply with USPAP?

USPAP states that when a signing appraiser relies on work done by others who do not sign the certification, the signing appraiser is responsible for the decision to rely on the trainee appraiser's work.

The name of the trainee appraiser who provided significant assistance, but does not sign the certification, must be stated in the certification. It is not required that the description of the assistance appear in the certification, but the extent of the assistance must be set forth in the report as required in STANDARDS 2, 3, 6, 8 and 10. The degree of this description is identified by the applicable reporting option for the assignment. For example, in an Appraisal Report, the extent of the significant assistance must be summarized.

Illustration 3

Advisory Opinion 31 – Illustration 3

Possession of Workfiles

(USPAP Advisory Opinions 2016-2017 Edition)

An appraiser is an employee of an appraisal firm. The firm has announced that the office is moving to another city. All appraisers not moving to the new location have been asked to turn over their workfiles to the company. The appraiser believes that he is required to keep the workfiles. Who is correct?

The RECORD KEEPING RULE does not mandate that an appraiser have possession of assignment workfiles. Employment contracts and other employment arrangements often require appraisers to leave their workfiles with an employer should the appraiser leave that firm, or in other situations. However, if an appraiser must relinquish actual possession of the workfiles, the appraiser must establish appropriate access arrangements for the length of the retention period. In the circumstances described, another solution may be for the appraiser to obtain permission from the employer to make copies of his or her workfiles.

Illustration 4

Advisory Opinion 31 – Illustration 4

Possession of Workfiles

(USPAP Advisory Opinions 2016-2017 Edition)

Jonathan is a trainee appraiser who has been working with the same supervising appraiser for some time. Recently, his supervising appraiser told him that since he was only a trainee, he had no right to access workfiles on appraisals where he had provided significant professional assistance. Is the supervising appraiser correct? Do trainees have any rights regarding access to workfiles?

*The supervising appraiser is not correct. USPAP places workfile retention requirements on the **appraiser**. Jonathan, since he is acting as an appraiser, is an appraiser as defined in USPAP. In assignments where more than one appraiser is involved (e.g., a trainee appraiser and a supervising appraiser,) each appraiser shares responsibility for complying with the RECORD KEEPING RULE.*

Illustration 4 (continued)

Supervising appraisers should be aware that all appraisers, including trainee appraisers, must maintain access to workfiles for a minimum of five years. A supervising appraiser must not impede a trainee appraiser's ability to access a workfile under the following conditions:

- Submission to state appraiser regulatory agencies;
- Compliance with due process of law;
- Submission to a duly authorized professional peer review committee; or
- Compliance with retrieval arrangements.

Denying access to a workfile that the trainee worked on is a violation of the ETHICS RULE. An individual appraiser employed by a group or organization that conducts itself in a manner that does not conform to these Standards should take steps that are appropriate under the circumstances to ensure compliance with the Standards.

Illustration 5

Advisory Opinion 31 – Illustration 5

Acknowledging Significant Appraisal Assistance

(USPAP Advisory Opinions 2016-2017 Edition)

Matthew, an appraiser, is working with a more senior appraiser on a complex appraisal assignment. His only task has been to develop the income approach based on information provided by the senior appraiser. What is the appropriate way to acknowledge Matthew's role in the assignment?

Since Matthew's work is limited to part of the assignment, signing a certification accepting responsibility for the entire assignment would not be appropriate. USPAP requires that Matthew be named in the certification, and the nature of his significant assistance be reported.

Illustration 6

Advisory Opinion 31 – Illustration 6

Acknowledging Significant Appraisal Assistance

(USPAP Advisory Opinions 2016-2017 Edition)

Margaret is performing a specific portion of a complex appraisal assignment, but is not competent to complete the entire assignment. As part of her training, she read the report and discussed it with the senior appraiser. Having now expanded her knowledge of the assignment, she wants to sign the certification along with the senior appraiser on the project. Is this appropriate?

No. By signing the certification, she would be accepting full responsibility for all elements of the certification, for the assignment results, and for the contents of the appraisal report. Although she was competent to perform her assigned task, reading the report and discussing it with the senior appraiser does not confer competence. Therefore, she cannot accept full responsibility for the assignment results or sign the certification.

Chapter Summary

1. STANDARD 1 establishes a benchmark of criteria for measuring ethics and competency in the development process and contains six Standards Rules (1-1 through 1-6) that identify applicable requirements and guidance for developing an appraisal of real property.

2. STANDARD 2 addresses the obligations of an appraiser for reporting a real property appraisal.

3. The names of individuals providing significant real property appraisal assistance who do not sign a certification must be stated in the certification. It is not required that the description of their assistance be contained in the certification, but disclosure of their assistance is required in accordance with Standards Rule 2-2 (a)(vii) or (b)(vii), as applicable.

4. The Comment to Standards Rule 3-6 is very similar to that found in Standards Rule 2-3, with the exception that the Comment to Standards Rule 3-6 specifically warns that appraisal review is a completely different activity than cosigning a report, such as when a supervisory appraiser cosigns with a trainee.

5. AO-31 addresses the issue with clarification and guidance in the form of relevant USPAP references, record keeping requirements, certifications/signatures, and illustrations.

Chapter Quiz

1. *STANDARD 1 of USPAP establishes a benchmark of criteria for measuring _____ and _____ in the appraisal development process.*

   A. compliance; certification
   B. depth; detail
   C. ethics; competency
   D. methods; techniques

2. *An important point from STANDARD 1 of USPAP for trainee appraisers to remember is that an appraiser cannot simply maintain the skills and the knowledge they initially possessed; they must*

   A. accept assignments beyond their market area.
   B. always have a mentor for whom to rely upon.
   C. continuously improve their skills to remain proficient.
   D. meet with their scheduled training group to log joint discussion hours.

3. *According to the <u>Comment</u> accompanying the Introduction of STANDARD 2, the form, format, and style of a report are specific to the*

   A. development steps undertaken in the assignment.
   B. needs of intended users and appraisers.
   C. scope of work determined necessary in an assignment.
   D. type of property that is the subject of the appraisal.

4. *Standards Rule 2-1 contains general obligations for all written and oral real property appraisal reports, including a specific obligation that all _____ _____ used in the assignment must be clearly and accurately disclosed.*

   A. assumptions, extraordinary assumptions, hypothetical conditions, and limiting conditions
   B. confidential elements and the sources of confidential information
   C. data and verification sources
   D. non-appraiser personnel and administrative assistance

5. *The <u>Comment</u> for Standards Rule 2-2(a)(vii), for the Appraisal Report option, advises that when any portion of the work involves significant real property appraisal assistance, the appraiser must _____ the extent of that assistance.*

   A. detail
   B. discuss
   C. state
   D. summarize

6. *STANDARD 2 contains specific content requirements for a real property appraisal report. As an overall obligation, Standards Rule 2-1 requires that appraisal reports contain _____ to enable intended users to understand the report properly.*

   A. definitions of appraisal terms
   B. exhibits and photographs
   C. simple and common language
   D. sufficient information

7. *The <u>Comment</u> to Standards Rule 3-6 is very similar to that found in Standards Rule 2-3. The one exception is the <u>Comment</u> to Standards Rule 3-6, specifically warning that*

   A. appraisal review is a completely different activity than cosigning a report.
   B. no significant assistance may be disclosed in an appraisal review report.
   C. supervisors and trainees must take responsibility for the elements of the work being reviewed.
   D. trainees must always sign an appraisal review report.

8. *Advice issued by the ASB indicates that if a trainee appraiser is asked by his or her supervisory appraiser to make changes to assignment results that were developed by the trainee for which the trainee does not agree, the trainee must*

   A. disassociate himself or herself from the supervisory appraiser.
   B. include a statement to that effect in the report.
   C. not sign the certification or the report.
   D. notify the Appraisal Practices Board.

9. *For a Restricted Appraisal Report, in addition to naming those providing significant assistance in the certification, the extent of that assistance must be _____ in the report.*

   A. detailed
   B. discussed
   C. stated
   D. summarized

10. *Standards Rule 3-6 states that each _____ must contain its own signed certification.*

    A. Appraisal Review Report
    B. Letter of Transmittal
    C. Narrative Summary Report
    D. Scope of Work Designation

Chapter 5

Responsibilities and Rules for the Supervisor & Trainee

The responsibility of the supervisory appraiser for the work of one or more trainee appraisers is inherent in most professions. In this chapter, responsibilities included in the supervisory/trainee relationship will be identified and explored.

As in other professions, the supervisory appraiser is responsible for closely supervising the work of trainees, for the training and development of trainees, and for exercising judgment as to the level of work the appraisal trainee is capable of and competent to perform. The appraisal trainee, in turn, uses education, experience, and work product performed under the direction of the supervisory appraiser to achieve certification. Each party has certain defined responsibilities during the relationship.

This chapter will focus mainly on responsibilities regarding the ethical obligations of the supervisor and trainee. Highlighted and examined thoroughly in this chapter are the ETHICS RULE along with fair housing and fair lending practices.

Chapter Objectives

After completing this chapter, you will be able to:

- Describe the ethical obligations of supervisory appraisers and trainee appraisers as presented in the ETHICS RULE.

- Identify the responsibilities of supervisory appraisers and trainees revealed in fair housing and fair lending practices.

Advocacy Occurs when the appraiser is representing the cause or interest of another, regardless of whether the cause or interest may be contrary to the appraiser's beliefs, opinions, conclusions, or recommendations.

Appraisal Practice Valuation services performed by an individual acting as an appraiser, including but not limited to appraisal or appraisal review. *

Bias A preference or inclination that precludes an appraiser's impartiality, independence, or objectivity in an assignment. *

Confidential Information Information that is either (1) Identified by the client as confidential when providing it to an appraiser and that is not available from any other source; or (2) Classified as confidential or private by applicable law or regulation.*

Fraudulent Reporting A serious and intentional act which is often considered a criminal activity.

Gross Negligence Willful, extreme, or reckless behavior, beyond what would be expected from a reasonable person.

Valuation Services Services pertaining to aspects of property value. *

*USPAP 2016-2017 Edition

Key Terms

Building Upon Ethics and Competency

The foundation of the relationship of a supervisory appraiser and a trainee appraiser is rooted in ethical behavior and competent practices. During the course of the relationship, the supervisor must constantly promote and reinforce ethical **appraisal practice**, while the trainee gains competency from the supervisor's mentoring guidance, educational coursework, and progressive hands-on learning.

The supervising appraiser's role and responsibility is to provide oversight and guidance in order for the trainee appraiser to gain competency. Likewise, the trainee appraiser must be willing to open his or her mind to learning sound practices, through both education and practical application.

First, let's amplify important points expounded by the ETHICS RULE of USPAP, which we discussed previously. The understanding and application of these obligations are the responsibility of both the supervisory appraiser and the trainee appraiser.

The ETHICS RULE and Public Trust

The ETHICS RULE begins by reminding us of the foundational obligation that *an appraiser must promote and preserve the public trust inherent in appraisal practice by observing the highest standards of professional ethics.*

An appraiser must *never* lose sight of this important obligation. Each of the sections of the ETHICS RULE recites key foundational principles leading to sound appraisal practices.

√ ***Note:*** Appraisers must be familiar with elements of each section.

ETHICS RULE—<u>Conduct</u> Section

Obligations of the <u>Conduct</u> section of the ETHICS RULE regarding **general conduct** include:

- Appraisers must not engage in criminal conduct.

- Appraisers must always be impartial, objective, and independent, without accommodating personal interests.

- Appraisers must not willfully or knowingly violate the requirements of the RECORD KEEPING RULE.

The appraiser's obligation to not engage in criminal conduct should seem obvious and not require discussion. Of course, not every action by an appraiser deemed to be an ethical error would rise to the level of a criminal act, and intentional criminal activities by an appraiser are rare; they are the exception rather than the norm. However, there is certainly opportunity for an appraiser, especially one who is relatively new to the profession, to unwittingly become involved in criminal conduct and not realize it at the time.

Common examples where appraisers might become involved in criminal conduct might include mortgage fraud schemes, or appraisals that might involve the IRS or other government entities. An appraiser must *always* be particularly cautious of involuntarily becoming a participant in unsavory activities. These activities often lead to an appraiser being held guilty in the public's perception simply by association. When appraisers are questioned regarding their practices or a particular service they have provided, the appraiser's workfile is frequently summoned and reviewed as part of the investigatory or discovery process.

√ ***Note:*** In cases of an investigation being conducted by an appraisal regulatory authority, numerous appraisal workfiles might be reviewed by that authority.

The RECORD KEEPING RULE of USPAP, which was discussed previously, recites an appraiser's responsibilities regarding workfile content, custody, and retention. When the provisions of the RECORD KEEPING RULE are deliberately violated, it is also a violation of the ETHICS RULE. This is why the obligations of this rule are so important to supervisory appraisers and appraiser trainees.

The final point of general conduct, which has intentionally been left for last, is the issue of independence, impartiality, and unbiased behavior on the part of the appraiser. The ETHICS RULE requires an appraiser to be independent and impartial, and prohibits **bias** when acting as an appraiser.

Appraiser bias, independence, and impartiality are areas of conduct that are often cited in complaints dealing with unacceptable appraisal behavior, and can be very broad in nature. Prohibitions regarding such behavior have been part of USPAP since its creation. Whether intentional or unintentional, some appraisers continue to cross the line. While a few appraisers may still permit their independence and impartiality to be influenced, the occurrence is less than in the past. The primary reason for this decline is new laws, regulations, and other provisions related to the mortgage lending industry that prohibit an appraiser from being influenced when providing an appraisal.

Numerous entities at the federal and state level, as well as nearly all mortgage lending participants (such as Fannie Mae, the FHA, the VA, and others) have enacted regulations prohibiting a party from attempting to influence an appraiser. Federal and state laws have been instituted as well to prevent such attempts. While each prohibition can vary somewhat, the general prohibition found in many state regulations is something similar to this:

> *1090.5. (a) No person with an interest in a real estate transaction involving an appraisal shall improperly influence or attempt to improperly influence, through coercion, extortion, or bribery, the development, reporting, result, or review of a real estate appraisal sought in connection with a mortgage loan. (The above prohibition) does not prohibit a person with an interest in a real estate transaction from asking an appraiser to do any of the following:*
>
> *(1) Consider additional, appropriate property information.*
>
> *(2) Provide further detail, substantiation, or explanation for the appraiser's value conclusion.*
>
> *(3) Correct errors in the appraisal report.*

Contrary to popular belief by many in the appraisal and lending industry, a lender or other party related to a transaction or property may interact with an appraiser. Caution must be taken, however, that discussions do not become inappropriate. Because of the potential risk, many lenders have established policy prohibiting their staff and associates from directly having discussion with an appraiser.

Conduct Section—Development Issues

Obligations of the <u>Conduct</u> section of ETHICS RULE regarding **development issues** include:

- *Appraisers must not perform an assignment with bias.*

- *Appraisers must not advocate for the cause or interest of any party or issue.*

- *Appraisers must not accept assignments that include reporting predetermined opinions and conclusions.*

- *Appraisers must not misrepresent their role when providing **valuation services** outside of appraisal practice.*

- *Appraisers must not perform assignments in a grossly negligent manner.*

The term advocacy is not included in the USPAP DEFINITIONS, while the term bias is. USPAP defines **bias** as: *A preference or inclination that precludes an appraiser's impartiality, independence, or objectivity in an assignment.* When an appraiser advocates for his client or a particular issue, the appraiser is *not* acting impartially. **Advocacy** *occurs when the appraiser is representing the cause or interest of another, regardless of whether the cause or interest may be contrary to the appraiser's beliefs, opinions, conclusions, or recommendations.*

An appraiser can **never advocate the cause or interest of any party or issue** and must **always** remain impartial (not favoring one side over the other) and objective; much like a judge would in a court case. In other professional roles, an individual may be **required** to advocate for their client. This is one major area where the ethical obligations of an appraiser differ from most other professions. For example, real estate brokers typically must advocate for their client's position and interest, similar to the duties expected of an attorney or certain other professionals when representing their clients.

One of the questions appraisers often ask out of concern for ethical compliance is "May I appraise a property that is owned by a friend or relative?" USPAP doesn't directly address the issue, other than to warn that **bias is not allowed when acting in the role of an appraiser**. As well, USPAP reporting obligations require that in the report certification, the appraiser must certify whether or not the appraiser has any personal interest with respect to the parties involved.

Appraisers must use special caution in circumstances where personal inclinations or preferences might cause assignment results to be biased. As well, an appraiser must give thought to how the practice might be perceived. For instance, could the appraiser defend appraising a property for a friend or relative and convince others that he was totally impartial if it were called into question?

Fair Housing and Fair Lending Practices

The <u>Conduct</u> section of the ETHICS RULE also addresses an appraiser's obligation to fair housing and fair lending practices. This is an area that is not often expanded upon during a trainee's education, but is especially important for sound practice. Appraisers must be particularly cautious regarding accusations of impropriety in this area as the consequences can be severe. Also, in most cases, E & O Insurance providers will **not** provide defense or coverage for such violations.

Appraisers must not use or rely on unsupported conclusions regarding characteristics related to specifically recognized protected classes, or an unsupported conclusion indicating that homogeneity of such characteristics is necessary to maximize value.

As mentioned earlier, protected classes or related characteristics of those classes that are indicated in USPAP include:

- Race
- Marital status
- Color
- Familial status
- Religion
- Age
- National origin
- Receipt of public assistance income
- Gender
- Handicap

Next, we will examine what Advisory Opinion 16 says about fair housing.

Fair Housing and Fair Lending Practices—USPAP Advisory Opinion 16

USPAP Advisory Opinion 16 addresses compliance with fair housing laws in the development and reporting of an appraisal. The BACKGROUND of the advisory opinion provides helpful insight, stating in part:

> *Fair housing law(s) preclude the use of certain specific information or supported conclusions related to protected group(s) in some assignments. Accordingly, an appraiser should be knowledgeable about the laws that affect the subject property of an assignment. Laws and regulations on fair lending and fair housing (such as the Fair Housing Act; the Equal Credit Opportunity Act (ECOA), and the laws and regulations of applicable federal, state, and local jurisdictions) continue to evolve. Further, appraisers must continue to provide appraisals that do not illegally discriminate or contribute to illegal discrimination.*

The BACKGROUND of Advisory Opinion 16 goes on to acknowledge, in part:

> *In some cases, even **supported** conclusions in assignments relating to characteristics such as race, color, religion, national origin, gender, marital status, familial status, age, receipt of public assistance income, handicap, or group homogeneity cannot be used because they are precluded by applicable law.*

USPAP Advisory Opinion 16 cites several examples that require specific research and competency to avoid the use of unsupported conclusions in the section labeled <u>Competency</u>. Cited examples include:

- *The property is designed to suit the needs of a protected group.*

- *There is little or no transaction information available on similar properties.*

- *The property is in a market setting where similar properties have not previously existed.*

- *Market conditions are not similar to the conditions prevailing during the time frame in which previous market transactions occurred.*

- *There are financially subsidized rental or ownership programs.*

The following illustrations are reproduced from Advisory Opinion 16.

AO-16—Illustration 1

An appraiser is completing an assignment in an area where crime activity has recently been publicized. The appraiser considers the use of the term "high-crime area." This is a subjective term that may be understood by the appraiser but may mislead the client. This term does not provide the evidence that the appraiser used in making the observation. The appraiser may provide a specific reference that is factual and objective (e.g., one crime per 100 people or one crime per 1,000,000 people) but may still mislead the client.

If the appraiser is to be competent with these types of statistics, the crime ratio should be correlated to the actions of the market in reflecting a valuation adjustment or other indication of property demand. If all of the comparables used by the appraiser are from a market sharing the same crime characteristic, the appraiser should question whether the term and/or the statistic(s) are relevant to the appraisal assignment.

AO-16—Illustration 2

A religious organization requests an appraiser to determine if a facility offering unique services to specific religious members is feasible. The appraiser must research a geographic market and identify concentrations of individuals that are members of that specific religion. Is the appraiser permitted to complete the assignment under USPAP?

The assignment is not covered by ECOA or the Fair Housing Act. Under USPAP, the appraiser must comply with the ETHICS RULE concerning discrimination. The key in this case is not to use or rely on unsupported conclusions. If the appraiser can identify the market behavior of the religious members and relate that behavior to the assignment, the appraiser is not in violation of USPAP.

AO-16—Illustration 3

An appraiser is requested to review a portfolio of apartment appraisal reports in a market area where apartments with public rent subsidies also exist. How does the <u>Conduct</u> section of the ETHICS RULE affect the appraisal reviewer's actions?

The review and conclusion of acceptance or rejection of the reports should not rely on the appraisal reviewer's unsupported conclusions regarding public assistance projects.

AO-16—Illustration 4

An appraiser is requested to appraise a house with specific features (e.g., ramps, wider doorways, and special plumbing fixtures) designed to accommodate handicapped individuals. How does the appraiser analyze the unique improvements?

The appraiser should reflect market preferences for the components of the structure. However, the appraiser should not draw an unsupported conclusion that the fixtures either enhance or diminish value.

USPAP FAQ

A USPAP Frequently Asked Question (FAQ) titled Use of Qualitative Terms also touches on fair housing/fair lending issues. In answer to whether or not an appraiser may use qualitative terms in an appraisal report, USPAP does NOT prohibit the use of such qualitative terms in an appraisal report. However, the <u>Conduct</u> section of the ETHICS RULE states:

An appraiser must not use or rely on unsupported conclusions relating to characteristics such as race, color, religion, national origin, gender, marital status, familial status, age, receipt of public assistance income, handicap, or an unsupported conclusion that homogeneity of such characteristics is necessary to maximize value.

Appraisers should exercise care to avoid comments in a report that may be perceived as biased or illegally discriminatory. Factual descriptions and qualitative terms allow the user of a report to draw his or her own conclusions. The use of terms that reflect a scale such as high, low, good, fair, poor, strong, weak, rapid, slow, average, or the like should also provide contextual information that properly explains the frame of reference and relative position of the subject property on the scale.

This FAQ also reminds us that any rating used by an appraiser should be accompanied by an explanation sufficient for intended users to understand the rating in the proper context. In a practical sense, and in keeping with defensible appraisal practices, an appraiser should always consider whether any element of discussion or reporting could be misleading, and that the report is clear and understandable. For example: Why are market conditions stable? Why is the subject property's physical condition stated as good? If absorption is stated as rapid, the context of the rating should also be cited (rapid relative to what?).

√ **Note:** Additional guidance is provided in Advisory Opinion 16, *Fair Housing Laws and Appraisal Report Content*.

Fair Housing and Fair Lending Practices: Negligent Practice

Other development issues included with the <u>Conduct</u> section of the ETHICS RULE include issues regarding appraisers misrepresenting their role when providing a valuation service, and performing in a grossly negligent manner. An example of an individual who could perform a valuation service in the role of either a real estate broker or as an appraiser was illustrated earlier.

Gross negligence is not specifically defined by USPAP. In practical terms, **gross negligence** typically implies *willful, extreme, or reckless behavior, beyond what would be expected from a reasonable person.* Appraisers, in avoiding the appearance of gross negligence, should be cautious that all due diligence determined necessary in the scope of work is performed.

<u>Conduct</u> Section: Reporting Issues

Obligations of the <u>Conduct</u> section of the ETHICS RULE regarding **reporting issues** include that an appraiser must **not**:

- Communicate assignment results with the intent to mislead or defraud.

- Communicate, use, or allow an employee or others to use a fraudulent or misleading report.

It should be obvious what is meant by reporting with the intent to mislead or defraud. **Fraudulent reporting** is, in most cases, a *serious and intentional act which is often considered a criminal activity.* Intentional misleading by the appraiser in an appraisal report could be intentional contortion of certain aspects of the report.

Sometimes, fraudulent reporting is done to favor the cause of the client (e.g., indicating the market is stable when it is actually declining). Other times, this might be an attempt by the appraiser to "sugar coat" certain property characteristics to avoid offending the property owner or others (e.g., not disclosing quality or condition aspects of a property). Appraisers should carefully survey their reporting components to assure that the commentary and conclusions presented (or lack of commentary) can be defended and are credible.

An appraiser's obligation to not communicate, use, or allow an employee or others to use a fraudulent or misleading report is somewhat broad, as it applies to *not only the appraiser*, but *also to others* **not** to communicate or use a report that is known to be fraudulent or misleading. When a client furnishes a copy of a previous appraisal to an appraiser in a subsequent assignment, if that appraiser finds misleading or fraudulent aspects in the previous report, he has a duty to inform the client of the misleading or fraudulent aspects. And, of course, while it is not unethical for the appraiser to read the previous report, he must not use or rely on the report in his assignment due to its misleading or fraudulent content.

The Conduct section of the ETHICS RULE concludes with obligations regarding the interest of the appraiser with regard to the subject property or the parties involved, and certain prior services by the appraiser.

The following information must be disclosed to the client *if known prior to accepting an assignment*, or *if discovered at any time during an assignment*:

- Any current or prospective interest in a subject property or the parties involved in the assignment.

- Any services as an appraiser, or in any other capacity, regarding the subject property, performed *within a three-year period prior* immediately preceding acceptance of the assignment.

In addition to the disclosure made prior to accepting the assignment, or one made if discovered any time during an assignment, **disclosure must be made in the certification** of the subsequent report. Disclosing prior services is important to preserving public trust, and it gives the client an opportunity to evaluate the information before engaging the appraiser. If the appraiser has agreed with a client in a previous assignment to not disclose that she performed that appraisal, the appraiser **must decline all assignments that fall within the three-year period**.

The Comment to this portion of the Conduct section of the ETHICS RULE provides specific advice regarding how these requirements interact with the appraiser's obligation of confidentiality:

> *Comment: Disclosing the fact that the appraiser has previously appraised the property is permitted except in the case when an appraiser has agreed with the client to keep the mere occurrence of a prior assignment confidential. If an appraiser has agreed with a client not to disclose that he or she has appraised a property, the appraiser must decline all subsequent assignments that fall within the three year period.*

The disclosure of prior services must be made in the certification of the report, stating whether or not a prior service was provided. When determining compliance of an appraisal report with USPAP, reviewers and regulatory investigators often check for compliance in this area first.

Apply Your Knowledge #1

1. If an appraiser has NOT provided any services regarding the subject property within the prior three years, does the <u>Conduct</u> section of the ETHICS RULE require an appraiser to disclose that no prior service has been performed?

    _____
    _____
    _____
    _____
    _____
    _____

2. Arthur has appraised a particular property four times in the past three years. He has just received another appraisal request for the same property. Is Arthur required to disclose the number of times that he has appraised the property in the previous three years, or just that he has performed an appraisal of the property in the previous three years?

    _____
    _____
    _____
    _____
    _____
    _____

3. Jason is a real property appraiser, who also operates a side business designing and crafting custom stained-glass windows. He has been offered an appraisal assignment of a residential property for which he was contracted to install several stained-glass windows two years ago. Jason understands that he must disclose that he has performed a prior service for the subject property within the past three years. Is Jason required to describe the specific service or merely that a service was performed?

    _____
    _____
    _____
    _____
    _____
    _____

4. John, a real property appraiser, appraised a high-end residential property two years ago. He was engaged in the assignment by the property's owner, a high profile individual. At the time of the assignment, the property owner required John to sign a confidentiality agreement with several prohibitions, for a period of five years, including disclosure of the fact that John had appraised the property. John is offered an appraisal assignment of the property by a national bank. Can John accept the assignment for a different client?

    _____
    _____
    _____
    _____
    _____

5. Craig is employed as a staff appraiser by a company who uses Craig's appraisals only for their internal use. In performing his duties, Craig only works on assignments for his employer, who is the client in the assignments, and does not accept assignments from outside parties. Since Craig only performs appraisal services for his employer, does he still need to disclose any previous appraisal or service provided within the previous three years, since his employer already knows this?

_____

_____

_____

_____

_____

_____

6. Monique is a residential appraiser who primarily works for lenders who specify that appraisals performed by her for their use be communicated using common reporting forms developed by Fannie Mae and Freddie Mac. The instructions for completing these forms prohibit any modifications to the certification, which is self-contained in the form. How can Monique comply with the _Conduct_ section of the ETHICS RULE, which requires disclosure of whether or not a prior service was performed regarding the subject property at the time of the assignment and in the report certification, and still use the pre-printed forms specified by the client?

_____

_____

_____

_____

_____

7. A few months ago, Jessica completed the appraisal of a property that involved a proposed construction of a new residential dwelling. The appraisal was "subject to" completion of the proposed improvements. Now, the client has asked Jessica to perform a final inspection of the property to confirm that the improvements have been completed per the proposed specifications. Is the request for the final inspection considered a new assignment? If so, does Jessica need to disclose the prior appraisal completed a few months ago, even if this would be obvious to the client?

_____

_____

_____

_____

_____

ETHICS RULE—<u>Management</u> Section

The <u>Management</u> section of the ETHICS RULE addresses, in part:

- Disclosing fees, commissions, or things of value paid in connection with the procurement of an assignment.

- Unacceptable assignment conditions and compensation arrangements.

- Advertising/soliciting assignments in a false, misleading, or exaggerated manner.

- Affixing or authorizing the use of the appraiser's signature to certify recognition and acceptance of that appraiser's USPAP responsibilities in appraisal practice.

Looking more closely at each of these issues, the <u>Management</u> Section elaborates upon **disclosure of payments by the appraiser in relation to procuring an assignment** and communicates that *an appraiser must disclose that he or she paid a fee or commission, or gave a thing of value in connection with the procurement of an assignment.* This disclosure must be included in the certification and in any transmittal letter in which conclusions are stated.

It should be made clear that the USPAP obligation refers to payments being made *by the appraiser*, not to the appraiser. The value of the item given, or the amount of the payment made by the appraiser, does not require disclosure. Gifts or other things of value provided to a client as a "thank you" or other appreciation for business, in general, do *not* require the disclosure. While the disclosure of payments made by the appraiser for an appraisal assignment has not been a significant area of disciplinary action in the past, the advent of AMC's and other avenues of appraisal referral and work assignment brings new questions regarding compliance with the provision.

Consider the following scenario on the next screen and respond with your thoughts on compliance.

Apply Your Knowledge #2

1. *Residential appraiser, Joan, has been engaged by an Appraisal Management Company (AMC) that was acting as the duly authorized representative of the lender, who is their client. The AMC has instructed appraiser Joan to collect the appraisal fee from the property owner, who is the borrower in the lender's transaction. She is to keep her portion of the fee, negotiated at the time of the assignment, and forward the remainder of the amount collected from the property owner to the AMC. Further, the AMC has instructed appraiser Joan not to disclose the amount of the total fee, or the negotiated fee split between her and the AMC in the appraisal report. Are this arrangement and the prohibition of disclosing the arrangement by Joan in the appraisal report in compliance with USPAP?*

_____

_____

_____

_____

_____

Management Section: Assignment Conditions and Compromised Independence

One of the major focuses of the Management section of the ETHICS RULE is unacceptable assignment conditions. This, too, is a significant area of concern for appraiser compliance. This section of the rule recites:

An appraiser must not accept an assignment, or have a compensation arrangement for an assignment, that is contingent on any of the following:

- *the reporting of a predetermined result (e.g., opinion of value);*

- *a direction in assignment results that favors the cause of the client;*

- *the amount of a value opinion;*

- *the attainment of a stipulated result (e.g., that the loan closes, or taxes are reduced); or*

- *the occurrence of a subsequent event directly related to the appraiser's opinions and specific to the assignment's purpose.*

These are conditions for which the appraiser's independence has been compromised. As well, compensation arrangements that could encourage or reward unethical behavior are prohibited. The Conduct section of the ETHICS RULE also prohibits acceptance of an assignment with predetermined opinions and conclusions, which is considered as an unacceptable assignment.

Advisory Opinion 19: Unacceptable Assignment Conditions

Many of the scenarios of unacceptable assignment conditions are presented in **USPAP Advisory Opinion 19 (AO-19)**, which addresses unacceptable assignments and provides illustrations of how to handle these situations. The following Skill Checks will explore some of the scenarios presented in Advisory Opinion 19.

Apply Your Knowledge #3

The following four application questions will each present a client's request to their appraiser. After each scenario, explain why this would represent an unacceptable assignment condition for the appraiser.

1. *"We need comps for (property description) that will support a loan of $_____. Can you provide them?"* Why would this represent an unacceptable assignment condition?

_____
_____
_____
_____
_____

2. *"Sale Price: _____."* Why would this represent an unacceptable assignment condition?

_____
_____
_____
_____

Apply Your Knowledge #3 (continued)

3. *"Approximate (or Minimum) value needed: _____." "Amount needed: _____." "Owner's estimate of value: _____." Would any of these represent an unacceptable assignment condition?*

_____

_____

_____

_____

_____

4. *"If this property will not appraise for at least _____, stop and call us immediately." "Please call and notify if it is NOT possible to support a value at or above _____, BEFORE YOU PROCEED!!" Why would this represent an unacceptable assignment condition?*

_____

_____

_____

_____

_____

Management Section: Signatures

With regard to advertising, the <u>Management</u> section of the ETHICS RULE states, in part:

An appraiser must not advertise for or solicit assignments in a manner that is false, misleading, or exaggerated.

Finally, signature requirements are addressed in the <u>Management</u> section of the ETHICS RULE and specify that an appraiser must affix or authorize the use of his signature for the purpose of certifying recognition of his responsibilities under USPAP. An appraiser may authorize the use of his signature *only on* an *assignment-by-assignment* basis. This section of the rule also conveys a caveat that an appraiser must not affix the signature of another appraiser without the other appraiser's consent.

The <u>Comment</u> to this section of the rule advises that appraisers must exercise due care to prevent unauthorized use of their signature. And, so long as the appraiser exercises such care, the appraiser is **not** responsible for unauthorized use of his signature.

ETHICS RULE—Confidentiality Section

Because an appraiser always is dealing with confidential information, there is certainly risk of accidently or unintentionally disclosing the information. And, an appraiser might disclose information deemed confidential, simply because he has a loose tongue. This is often a temptation for appraisal trainees as they begin their practice. Regardless of the circumstances surrounding improper disclosure of confidential information, there is potential for action against an appraiser.

Many appraisers have difficulty defining what information is confidential and what is not. Before beginning discussion of the <u>Confidentiality</u> section of the ETHICS RULE, the USPAP definition of the term confidential information should be reviewed. USPAP defines **confidential information** as:

Information that is either:

- *Identified by the client as confidential when providing it to an appraiser and that is not available from any other source; or*

- *Classified as confidential or private by applicable law or regulation.*

The <u>Confidentiality</u> section of the ETHICS RULE addresses, in part:

- Protection of the confidential nature of the appraiser-client relationship.
- Acting in good faith with the legitimate interests of the client related to confidential information and in communicating assignment results.
- Obligation to be aware and to comply with all confidentiality laws and regulations applicable in an assignment.
- Disclosure requirements and exceptions to the protection of confidential information and assignment results.

The focus of the <u>Confidentiality</u> section of the ETHICS RULE is on the appraiser-client relationship and the use of confidential information and assignment results.

An appraiser must not disclose (1) confidential information; or (2) assignment results to anyone other than:

- *The client;*
- *Parties specifically authorized by the client;*
- *State appraiser regulatory agencies;*
- *Third parties as may be authorized by due process of law; or*
- *A duly authorized professional peer review committee except when such disclosure to a committee would violate applicable law or regulation.*

The <u>Comment</u> to this section of the rule specifies that when all elements of confidential information are removed through redaction or aggregation, client consent to disclose the remaining information as modified is not required. An important point that should be discussed is that there is no specified limitation on the length of time that an appraiser must keep information confidential. The appraiser has a responsibility to keep information confidential ***indefinitely***.

Keeping information confidential indefinitely is especially important for appraiser trainees. Sample reports sent to state appraisal regulatory agencies as part of the application process (or for any other reason) do not require client consent for their submission, nor does it necessitate redaction or aggregation. Also, appraiser trainees may, at some point, apply to an appraisal trade organization for membership or a designation, which might require submission of sample reports to a peer review committee. In such case, client consent or redaction/aggregation is not necessary as the peer review committee is comprised of appraisers. However, the committee must not violate confidentiality.

Apply Your Knowledge #4

1. *Barry, an appraiser, has applied for a professional designation of a major appraisal organization. As part of the approval process, Barry must submit sample appraisals reports for review by the designation committee of the organization. The committee is comprised of appraisers. Can Barry comply with USPAP and supply the sample reports?*

2. *While inspecting a subject property for an appraisal being performed for a lender-client, the homeowner has asked the appraiser to keep confidential certain information about the condition of the property in the appraisal report to the lender. Can the appraiser treat this information as confidential?*

√ **Note:** When all confidential elements of confidential information are removed through redaction or the process of aggregations, client authorization is not required for the disclosure of the remaining information, as modified.

Chapter Summary

1. During the course of the relationship, the supervisor must constantly promote and reinforce ethical appraisal practice, while the trainee gains competency from the supervisor's mentoring guidance, educational coursework, and progressive hands-on learning.

2. When the provisions of the RECORD KEEPING RULE are deliberately violated, it is also a violation of the ETHICS RULE.

3. Appraiser bias, independence, and impartiality are areas of conduct that are often cited in complaints dealing with unacceptable appraisal behavior.

4. An appraiser can never advocate the cause or interest of any party or issue and must always remain impartial.

5. Development issues included with the <u>Conduct</u> section of the ETHICS RULE include issues regarding appraisers misrepresenting their role when providing a valuation service, and performing in a grossly negligent manner.

6. Obligations of the <u>Conduct</u> section of the ETHICS RULE regarding reporting issues include that an appraiser must **not** communicate assignment results with the intent to mislead or defraud, or communicate, use, or allow an employee or others to use a fraudulent or misleading report.

7. Fraudulent reporting is, in most cases, a serious and intentional act which is often considered a criminal activity.

8. The <u>Management</u> Section elaborates upon disclosure of payments by the appraiser in relation to procuring an assignment and communicates that an appraiser must disclose that he or she paid a fee or commission, or gave a thing of value in connection with the procurement of an assignment.

9. An appraiser may authorize the use of his signature *only on* an *assignment-by-assignment* basis. This section of the rule also conveys a caveat that an appraiser must not affix the signature of another appraiser without the other appraiser's consent.

10. The appraiser has a responsibility to keep information confidential indefinitely.

Chapter Quiz

1. *Supervisory appraiser Gloria's client requested that she appraise a property that she has appraised twice in the past three years. Her trainee asks her what protocol she must follow in this situation. With this in mind, which statement is FALSE?*

    A. Gloria must disclose each prior service in the certification of the report.

    B. Gloria must disclose each prior service to the client.

    C. Gloria must make disclosure prior to accepting the assignment.

    D. Gloria must not disclose any prior service(s) in the latest assignment.

2. *Marcus, a trainee, is in the final months of his experience period and was just engaged to appraise a home that he had previously appraised along with his supervisor one year ago. May Marcus accept the assignment?*

    A. No, Marcus may not accept an assignment on the same property within three years of the prior assignment.

    B. No, since an appraisal was recently performed, Marcus may be biased about certain aspects of the home.

    C. Yes, Marcus may accept the assignment as long as he discloses the previous service on the property to the client and in the subsequent report certification.

    D. Yes, Marcus may accept the assignment as long as he does not disclose that he had previously appraised the property.

3. *Confidential information can be disclosed to parties specifically authorized by the client, state appraisal agencies, third parties as authorized by law, or a(n)*

    A. attorney at law.

    B. duly authorized professional peer review committee.

    C. party who paid for the appraisal.

    D. potential client who is using the information to place the appraiser on an "approved" list.

4. *If an appraiser indicates in his report to a client that the market is stable when it is declining, this is an example of*

    A. fraud for property.

    B. fraudulent reporting.

    C. property flipping.

    D. short sale fraud.

5. *A supervisory appraiser and his trainee are pressured to deliver an appraisal report. Because the client insists on receiving a value opinion today, they realize there is much research they did not have time to perform. This violates the Conduct section of the ETHICS RULE, specifying that an appraiser must NOT perform an assignment in a(n) _____ manner.*

    A. grossly negligent

    B. hurried

    C. improper

    D. offensive

6. *Which statement is FALSE regarding an appraiser performing an appraisal of a property owned by a friend or relative?*

    A. Appraisers must use caution in circumstances where personal inclinations might cause assignment results to be biased.

    B. A personal interest with the property or the parties involved must be disclosed in the report certification.

    C. USPAP doesn't directly address the issue, other than to warn that bias is not allowed when acting as an appraiser.

    D. USPAP specifically prohibits appraisal of property owned by family members or personal friends of the appraiser.

7. *Joseph is an appraiser undertaking the appraisal of a property which has specialized features for handicap accessibility. What should Joseph's next step be to determine the positive or negative value influence of such property features?*

    A. consider the features in context of objective market preferences

    B. include a nominal adjustment to affirm they were considered

    C. make a negative adjustment, as such features always diminish the value of a property

    D. value the property as if the features were not there

8. *If an appraiser states that the condition of a neighborhood is good, average, fair, etc., what should the appraiser also include with his or her rating?*

   A. a disclosure that the rating is the subjective opinion of the appraiser

   B. a discussion of the appraiser's qualifications to establish the rating

   C. an explanation that clarifies the rating in its proper context

   D. a statement that the rating is an extraordinary assumption

Chapter 6

General Responsibilities of the Supervisor/Trainee Relationship

Continuing the discussion from Chapter 5, this chapter will delve into the general responsibilities of the supervisor/trainee relationship. Fundamental obligations of the supervisory appraiser and trainee appraiser will be presented as well as the grounds for general compliance. Development and reporting responsibilities will also be represented to reveal proper assignment responsibilities. Valuation analysis and reporting responsibilities are discussed as are workfile obligations. All of the outlined responsibilities are critical in providing a thorough understanding of successful training for a novice appraiser.

Chapter Objectives

After completing this chapter, you will be able to:

- Define the specific responsibilities of supervisory appraisers.
- Identify the specific duties and responsibilities of trainee appraisers.
- Describe the assignment responsibilities required in general development and reporting.
- Identify valuation analysis and reporting responsibilities.

General Responsibilities of the Supervisor/Trainee Relationship

The appraisal experience period should be considered as a comprehensive education opportunity in which the supervisory appraiser reinforces ethical practices while assisting the trainee in gaining the competency necessary for his or her future success. The benchmark of a successful supervisory/trainee relationship is for the trainee to take away from the experience **the knowledge to provide appraisal services in an ethical and competent manner**. Of course, in order for trainees to effectively become ingrained in ethical and competent practices, the supervisory appraiser must himself possess ethical attributes and be competent to act as a supervisory appraiser.

Trainee appraisers have a responsibility to constantly assess the training they are being provided, and to be vigilant that the supervisory appraiser adheres to the highest level of professional standards. Supervisors have the responsibility to meet such expectations.

The supervisory appraiser is charged with a significant responsibility for the applied education and oversight of a trainee appraiser. Some responsibilities are more functional in nature, such as how to use particular appraisal software or the procedure for accessing certain data sources. But, the primary charge of a supervisory appraiser is to make certain trainees are doing things the right way.

Paramount of all responsibilities, prospective supervisory appraisers must self-assess that they possess the necessary ethical knowledge and sound habits of practice. As well, they must be competent to function as supervisory appraisers. The number of years in practice does not necessarily translate to the ability to adequately supervise a trainee. An appraiser who practices without adherence to professional ethics or without regard to competency is a very poor supervisory appraiser candidate.

Likewise, prospective supervisory appraisers must ensure that potential trainees hold a willingness to practice within the boundaries of professional ethics and competency.

Supervisory Appraiser Fundamental Obligations

The AQB and state regulatory rules set forth broad fundamental obligations for supervisor appraisers. Assuming the supervisory appraiser is sufficiently ethical and competent, the general responsibilities within that role include, but are not limited to:

- Assisting the trainee with gaining general market competence, including, locational, and physical characteristics
- Introducing the trainee to the various data sources typically used by appraisers in the market
- Instilling a basic understanding of USPAP requirements
- Ensuring the trainee is complying with USPAP
- Monitoring the trainee's progress through the experience and education process
- Continually overseeing and reviewing the development and reporting of each appraisal assignment
- Verifying proper documentation of the experience log
- Understanding the AQB's minimum supervisor/trainee requirements and specific state regulations
- Monitoring compliance with all national and state requirements for trainees
- Providing guidance to the trainee in their specific desired credentialing path
- Accompanying the trainee on all inspections until any state regulation has been satisfied and/or until the trainee is competent
- Providing duties and assignments that will ensure understanding, experience, and knowledge of all applicable valuation methodologies and approaches to value
- Suggesting additional education or courses in specialized topics specific to properties commonly found in the appraiser's market (i.e., historic homes, green construction, underground homes)
- Suggesting additional education or courses in topics to enhance the trainee's basic appraisal abilities (i.e., effective writing and communication skills, construction basics, organizational skills)

- Regularly meeting with the trainee to assess and discuss progress and actions to address any deficiencies
- Notifying the trainee appraiser if a circumstance arises where the supervisory appraiser is no longer qualified or able to supervise the trainee and/or sign the trainee's experience log

Supervisory Responsibilities in Assignments

A frequent complaint heard about supervisory appraisers is that the supervisor simply stands in the corner, or follows the trainee around during the site inspection, and then briefly peruses and rubber-stamps the appraisal report prepared by the trainee. And in some cases, the supervisor may not participate in the site inspection at all.

Of course, once the trainee demonstrates progressive competence, or meets the minimum requirements established by state regulation, the trainee may take more of an active role in both the inspection process and appraisal development and reporting. In either case, the supervisory appraiser holds a significant responsibility for the trainee's actions and performance.

For the purpose of this discussion, we will assume the supervisory appraiser and the trainee appraiser are in the infancy stage of their relationship and undertaking a real property appraisal of a single-family residential dwelling with an interior and exterior inspection. Of course, the procedure may be also applicable to other property types and appraisal services.

The purpose of this discussion is not to detail how property should be inspected or appraised, but rather the duties of the supervisory appraiser in the course of supervising his or her trainee. While the elements of the discussion can be used as a checklist for supervisor responsibilities, the steps in the process could also be applied by trainees as a benchmark of responsibility for sound practice.

Each site inspection performed by an appraiser trainee and overseen by a supervisory appraiser should be considered as an educational opportunity for the trainee. Most will agree that no two properties will be the same and each may present differing characteristics and appraisal challenges. Certainly, the supervisory appraiser and the trainee should review the scope of work in the assignment prior to the inspection.

Supervisors should ensure that the workfile, at this point, contains the appropriate property records and other documentation to properly identify the property being appraised. This information may include:

- Assessor's or auditor's property records
- Legal description
- Construction documents for any proposed improvements

Reviewing the appropriate property records and other documentation on-site with the trainee assists the trainee in recognizing physical characteristics, discrepancies, and legal considerations, such as observing easements, conditions that do not meet public or private regulations, etc. As well, the supervisory appraiser should review with the trainee any assignment conditions requiring specific inspection or reporting obligations.

Especially in the early stages of a trainee's experience, during the inspection process, it is a good practice for **both the supervisor and the trainee to take separate field notes**. The notes can then be compared so that the trainee may learn from any omissions he or she might have made. Regularly doing this will also assist the supervisory appraiser to recognize the trainee's growth in the inspection process.

Once the supervisory appraiser is satisfied the field notes and the data collected are thorough, and before leaving the property, the supervisor should also **review photographs** to assure they are acceptable in quality and meet any assignment conditions (assuming the photographs are digital).

Assignment Responsibilities – General Development and Reporting

There could be various acceptable ways for which the appraisal is developed, with a couple of possibilities being most common.

- The supervisory appraiser may solely develop the appraisal opinions and conclusions with the trainee assisting with all or part of the data research, or

- The trainee could be completing all research and analysis, forming opinions and conclusions on his or her own.

- With the first option with the supervisory appraiser solely developing the appraisal opinions and the *trainee assisting with data research*, the trainee is likely providing significant appraisal assistance, and will **probably not** sign the report certification.

- With the *trainee forming opinions and conclusions* in the second option, the supervisory appraiser and trainee will usually **each** sign the report certification.

In either case, regardless of the trainee's level of participation, by signing the report certification, **the supervisory appraiser is responsible for all elements of the assignment** (as is the trainee if he or she also signs the certification).

It is ultimately important that the supervisory appraiser **constantly monitor the work being done by the trainee.** Let's look at some of the particular steps the supervisory appraiser should take related to reviewing an appraisal report prepared by a trainee appraiser.

Depending upon the stage of the experience process and the competency demonstrated by the trainee, these important points may be surveyed by the supervisor periodically during the trainee's appraisal development process or all points may be reviewed upon the trainee presenting his written or draft report.

> √ **Note:** A supervisory appraiser reviewing a trainee appraiser's work is **not** considered an appraisal review under STANDARD 3 of USPAP.

If the supervisory appraiser is **reviewing a completed appraisal report or draft prepared by the trainee**, likely he or she will read the entire report and note the general contents for development and reporting compliance. For the ease of discussion, we will break down the supervisor's critique into three categories:

1. General Compliance
2. Valuation Analysis and Reporting
3. Workfile

Not all appraisal assignments will require the same development and reporting obligations – some may require more and some may require less. However, this discussion will focus on the most common development and reporting obligations found in most traditional assignments. Again, some of these responsibilities may have been satisfied as the appraisal assignment was being developed by the trainee.

General Compliance

In the category of **General Compliance**, most every element not directly associated with the approaches to value or the workfile have been included. Therefore, the list of supervisory responsibilities is lengthy.

The supervisor is responsible to ensure:

- The proper appraisal reporting option and format has been used and is appropriately labeled.

- The report is free of typographical and grammatical errors.

- Any assignment conditions have been addressed – for example, requirements of the Uniform Appraisal Dataset (UAD), special instructions regarding development and reporting of the valuation approaches, additional development and reporting elements.

- The scope of work determined necessary has been satisfied and sufficiently reported.
- Extraordinary assumptions and hypothetical conditions used in the assignment are properly disclosed with the appropriate warning that their use may have affected the assignment results.
- An opinion of reasonable exposure time linked to the value opinion has been developed and reported, when applicable.
- All subject information is accurate and correctly reported.
- The current contract and prior offering history of the subject property has been researched, analyzed, and reported.
- Subject neighborhood characteristics and market conditions have been sufficiently researched, analyzed, and reported, and conclusions are logical, appropriately supported, and documented.
- Subject neighborhood description is thorough and sufficient.
- Site characteristics, physical and legal, are accurate and adequately reported.
- The highest and best use of the subject property is stated, and the rationale for that opinion is summarized in the report.
- All improvements have been sufficiently noted and ratings for functional utility, condition, and quality are not contrary to the estimated effective age.
- Estimated effective age is logical, supported, and adequately explained in the report.
- Other site improvements have been recognized and reported.
- All appropriate addenda, attachments, and exhibits are included within the report.
- The extent of the trainee's significant appraisal assistance is noted in the report, if the trainee is not signing the certification.
- Appropriate certification statements have been added when necessary, such as (but not limited to) a statement regarding prior services and disclosure of significant appraisal assistance (if trainee is not signing the certification).

Valuation Analysis and Reporting

In the category of **Valuation Analysis and Reporting**, the supervisory appraiser is responsible to critique the development and reporting of the approaches to value and their respective indications, as well as the final reconciliation of value. The supervisory appraiser is likely to spend a **significant amount of time** in this area, especially the sales comparison approach and the final reconciliation, in most assignments. So, our discussion will start there.

Valuation Analysis and Reporting – Sales Comparison Approach

Only in very rare instances is the **sales comparison approach** *not* developed as a part of most assignments. While all areas of development and reporting are important for the supervisory appraiser to thoroughly review, the supervisor should review the development and reporting of the sales comparison approach *with extra diligence*. Even in assignments where other approaches to value have been developed, the sales comparison approach is most often used as a primary indicator of value. When examined closely in review, the data, analysis, and conclusions reached in the methodology are often found to be the culprit for poor assignment results.

At a minimum, the supervisory appraiser should examine the sales comparison approach to ensure the:

- Best comparable data has been chosen.
- Data sources for comparable data are verified correctly.
- Subject and comparable information have been correctly reported.
- Adjustments have been applied when necessary and are consistent.
- Adjustments are supported and reasonable.
- Adjustments have been applied in the correct direction (plus or minus).

- Math applied is correct.
- Net and gross adjustments are accurate.
- Transfer history of the subject and comparable sales is accurate, thoroughly analyzed, and sufficiently reported.
- Summary of the sales comparison approach is logical, understandable, and thorough.
- Summary of the sales comparison approach includes reasoning for any inconsistent application of adjustments for differences between the subject and comparable properties, or the reasoning no adjustment was applied.
- Summary of the sales comparison approach includes discussion of the scope of research and analysis, including the reasoning for not using comparable data that might be considered relevant by the client or other intended users, or the information is contained in the workfile.
- Discussion includes the methodology used for deriving adjustments.
- Reconciliation is logical and the rationale for the conclusion is reasonable and fully supported.

√ **Note:** The reasoning for exclusion of the sales comparison approach must be explained if it was not developed.

Valuation Analysis and Reporting – Cost Approach

While not developed as often as the sales comparison approach in many appraisals, the **cost approach** is developed in many assignments, either as a result of *its relevance or due to assignment conditions* specified by the client. When the cost approach is developed and reported, the supervisory appraiser has a responsibility to see that the conclusions in the development are credible, and that the reporting is complete and understandable.

The supervisory appraiser should observe the:

- Methodology for estimating site value has been explained and/or presented.
- Source(s) and rationale for estimating cost new of the improvements is presented/discussed.
- Methodology for depreciation is addressed and that the depreciation assigned is consistent with the effective age and remaining economic life.
- As-is value of other site improvements is reasonable and the rationale is explained or contained in the workfile.
- Reconciliation is logical and the rationale for the conclusion is reasonable and fully supported.

√ **Note:** The reasoning for exclusion of the cost approach must be explained if it was not developed.

Valuation Analysis and Reporting – Income Approach

Again, there will be select situations warranting the development and reporting of the **income approach**. When development of the methodology is *necessary for credible assignment results*, there are a number of elements the appraisal report must evidence, which must be observed by the supervisory appraiser.

The supervisor is responsible to ensure the:

- The terms of any existing lease or rental agreement is discussed.
- Potential income of the property is supported and discussed, or contained in the workfile.
- Estimated vacancy rate and collection loss are supported and discussed, or contained in the workfile.
- Expense estimates are supported and discussed, or contained in the workfile.

- Derivation of rates of capitalization (GRM, GIM, overall capitalization rate) is discussed or illustrated, or contained in the workfile.
- Reconciliation is logical and the rationale for the conclusion is reasonable and fully supported.

> √ **Note:** Depending upon the particular income technique used, **not all elements may be applicable.**

Valuation Analysis and Reporting – Final Reconciliation

Many appraisals fall short in the **final reconciliation** of value. The supervisory appraiser must carefully review the reconciliation in the report to make certain the:

- Report correctly reflects the conditions for the value opinion (as-is or subject-to).
- Reasonableness and reliability of each applicable approach to value has been reconciled.
- Reasonableness and validity of the indicated value has been reconciled.
- Reasonableness of the available data has been reconciled.
- Report contains discussion and rationale for the valuation approach or approaches that were given the most weight.
- Report contains the logic and rationale for the data that was used and the approaches that were developed.

The final reconciliation should paint a clear picture of the logic and rationale used in concluding on a particular value opinion. Never should the reader be left to question the reasoning of an appraiser to arrive at a certain value opinion.

Workfile

Finally, the supervisory appraiser has the responsibility to review the workfile for compliance with USPAP and any other regulations applicable to the appraiser or to the assignment. The obligations of the RECORD KEEPING RULE of USPAP were discussed previously.

The supervisory appraiser has the responsibility to **examine the workfile** to ensure it contains:

- A true signed copy of the written report submitted to the client (or required documents for an oral report).
- All field notes.
- Property records relied upon in the assignment.
- Construction plans, estimates, documents if the subject assignment includes proposed construction, renovations, or repairs (or the location of the information if not contained in the workfile).
- Additional documentation for data used and data not used in the approaches to value.
- Calculations and worksheets for costs, adjustments, etc. relative to the valuation approaches.
- Names and contact information of outside individuals interviewed or consulted in the assignment.
- Other documentation related to the appraiser's engagement, which includes the name of the client and the name or type of other intended users.
- Sufficient information to produce an appraisal report (if the Restricted Appraisal reporting option was used in the assignment).

> √ **Caution!** Supervisory appraisers and trainee appraisers must also be mindful of the record keeping requirements regarding workfile custody, access, retrieval, and retention, which were discussed in previous chapters.

Specific Responsibilities of the Trainee Appraiser

Thus far in the discussion of responsibilities, the focus has been on specific supervisory appraiser duties and responsibilities within assignments for compliance by both the supervisory appraiser and the trainee appraiser. However, there are some very specific responsibilities to which trainee appraisers must comply.

Trainees have the **responsibility to have a basic understanding** of:

- The minimum requirements to become a trainee appraiser set forth by the AQB, and

- Any requirements established by state appraisal regulatory authorities, which may be greater.

Trainees have the responsibility to determine that *a prospective supervisory appraiser is qualified and in good standing.* Sources for the trainee to check include the Appraisal Subcommittee (ASC) National Registry and state appraisal regulatory agencies websites.

√ **Note:** Seeking out a supervisory appraiser with the experience and competency best matching the trainee appraiser's credentialing path is the *responsibility of the trainee.*

Trainees also have a responsibility to recognize that *their relationship and experience potential under the oversight of a supervisory appraiser is directly connected to the good standing of the supervisory appraiser.* In other words, if action is taken against the supervisory appraiser that would affect the supervisor's credential to be suspended or revoked, the trainee **cannot** practice and earn experience credit under that individual's supervision.

Trainee appraisers have a responsibility to *understand the importance of selecting an appropriate supervisory appraiser and are expected to recognize that the supervisor/trainee relationship is a long-term relationship.* In order for continued uninterrupted growth to occur, the best circumstance for that learning environment is one in which both the supervisor and the trainee consistently gain an understanding and respect.

The trainee is responsible to understand that *the supervisory appraiser has the duty to monitor the trainee's performance as well as the trainee's education and experiential learning* necessary to the trainee appraiser's specific credentialing path.

The trainee appraiser is responsible to understand that *the supervisory appraiser has the duty to provide assignments and tasks that sufficiently ensure the trainee is developing an understanding and progression of knowledge,* which includes experience of all applicable valuation methodologies and approaches to value.

It is the responsibility of the trainee to understand that *the supervisory appraiser must accompany him on all inspections until the trainee is competent to conduct the inspection on his own, and has met all of the requirements mandated by state appraisal regulatory authorities.*

The trainee has the responsibility to understand that *both the supervisory appraiser and the trainee appraiser have a joint duty to properly document all appropriate trainee appraiser's experience logs.*

Finally, the trainee appraiser has the responsibility to *recognize when the supervisory appraiser is no longer qualified to serve in a supervisory capacity.* When the supervisory appraiser is, for any reason, no longer qualified to serve in that capacity, no further qualifying experience may be earned under that individual. In such case, the trainee appraiser must be prepared to seek out a new qualified supervisory appraiser with whom he may resume gaining experience and earning qualifying hours.

√ **Note:** Supervisory appraisers also have the duty to notify the trainee appraiser when they are no longer qualified.

Chapter Summary

1. The benchmark of a successful supervisory/trainee relationship is for the trainee to take away from the experience the knowledge to provide appraisal services in an ethical and competent manner

2. Prospective supervisory appraisers must self-assess that they possess the necessary ethical knowledge and sound habits of practice.

3. Supervisory appraisers are fundamentally obligated to assist trainees with gaining general market competence, oversee and review the development and reporting of each appraisal assignment, provide guidance to the trainee, accompany the trainee on all inspections until the trainee is competent, instill a basic understanding of USPAP, and monitor the trainee's progress through the experience and education process.

4. The supervisor and the trainee should take separate field notes as a general practice to compare and contrast for educational purposes.

5. Regardless of the trainee's level of participation, by signing the report certification, the supervisory appraiser is responsible for all elements of the assignment, as is the trainee if he or she also signs the certification.

6. A supervisory appraiser's review of a completed appraisal report or draft prepared by the trainee should include a critique broken down into (1) General Compliance, (2) Valuation Analysis and Reporting, and (3) the Workfile.

7. In the category of General Compliance, most every element not directly associated with the approaches to value or the workfile should be included.

8. In the category of Valuation Analysis and Reporting, the supervisory appraiser is responsible to critique the development and reporting of the approaches to value and their respective indications, as well as the final reconciliation of value.

9. Trainees have the responsibility to have a basic understanding of the minimum requirements to become a trainee appraiser set forth by the AQB, and any requirements established by state appraisal regulatory authorities, which may be greater.

10. Trainees have a responsibility to recognize that their relationship and experience potential under the oversight of a supervisory appraiser is directly connected to the good standing of the supervisory appraiser.

Chapter Quiz

1. *Which is NOT necessary to be a responsible supervisory appraiser?*

    A. competency to function in that role
    B. extensive number of years as a certified appraiser
    C. knowledge of ethical obligations
    D. sound habits of practice

2. *Which statement regarding trainee appraiser responsibilities is TRUE?*

    A. Potential trainees are expected to possess knowledge and experience prior to becoming a trainee.
    B. Trainee appraisers must recognize that a supervisory appraiser must accompany them on all inspections for the duration the experience period.
    C. Trainee appraisers are expected to secure several supervisory appraisers to gain necessary competency.
    D. Trainees have the responsibility to understand that both the supervisor and the trainee have a joint duty for documentation of experience logs.

3. *Which is a source trainees may reference to determine if a prospective supervisory appraiser is qualified and in good standing?*

    A. Appraisal Institute
    B. Appraisal Standards Board
    C. Appraisal Subcommittee
    D. Appraiser Qualifications Board

4. *A supervisory appraiser has the responsibility to examine a workfile for all of the following EXCEPT*

    A. data not used in the approaches to value
    B. field notes
    C. trainee credentials
    D. worksheets for costs relative to the valuation approach.

5. *When reviewing an appraisal report prepared by a trainee, it is the responsibility of the supervisory appraiser to observe that any extraordinary assumptions or hypothetical conditions used in the assignment are*

    A. addressed in the report certification.
    B. consented to by the client.
    C. disclosed with the appropriate warning.
    D. an element of the original scope of work.

6. *Which is a responsible property inspection practice for a supervisory appraiser who will assist in recognizing the trainee's growth in the inspection process?*

    A. allow the trainee to perform inspections without the presence of the supervisor
    B. joint inspection by the supervisor and the trainee, with each taking separate notes
    C. separate, non-simultaneous inspections by both the trainee and the supervisor
    D. supervisory appraiser observes but does not participate in the inspection

7. *In regard to the approaches to value, a responsibility of the supervisory appraiser, when one or more of the approaches to value has not been developed, is to ensure the trainee has*

    A. at a minimum, drafted the approach, and included it in the workfile.
    B. explained the reasoning for not developing the approach(es).
    C. gained consent from the client to omit the approach(es).
    D. used an extraordinary assumption regarding the omission.

8. *Which is a TRUE statement regarding responsibility when a supervisory appraiser is no longer qualified to supervise a trainee appraiser?*

    A. It is the responsibility of the supervisory appraiser to identify a replacement.
    B. A notice is provided to the trainee by the Appraisal Subcommittee.
    C. The supervisory appraiser must notify the trainee if he is no longer qualified.
    D. Trainees can continue to practice until a new supervisory appraiser is found.

Glossary

Advocacy Occurs when the appraiser is representing the cause or interest of another, regardless of whether the cause or interest may be contrary to the appraiser's beliefs, opinions, conclusions, or recommendations.

The Appraisal Foundation (TAF) A nonprofit private organization which is recognized by Congress as the authority for professional appraisal standards and appraiser qualifications.

Appraisal Practice Valuation services performed by an individual acting as an appraiser, including but not limited to appraisal or appraisal review. *

Appraisal Practices Board An independent board of The Appraisal Foundation which is responsible for identifying and issuing opinions on Recognized Valuation Methods and Techniques, which may apply to all disciplines within the appraisal profession.

Appraisal Standards Board (ASB) An independent board of The Appraisal Foundation which is responsible for the subject, style, content, and substance of USPAP and other communications related to appraisal standards, including Advisory Opinions and FAQs.

Appraisal Subcommittee Created as a result of the Financial Institutions Reform, Recovery, and Enforcement Act (FIRREA) to provide federal oversight of State appraiser regulatory programs and a monitoring framework for the Appraisal Foundation and the Federal Financial Institutions Regulatory Agencies in their roles to protect federal financial and public policy interests in real estate appraisals utilized in federally related transactions.

Appraiser's Peers Other appraisers who have expertise and competency in a similar type of assignment. *

Appraiser Qualifications Board (AQB) An independent board of The Appraisal Foundation which is responsible for establishing minimum education, experience, and other criteria for certification and recertification of qualified appraisers.

Assignment Results An appraiser's opinions and conclusions developed specific to an assignment. *

Bias A preference or inclination that precludes an appraiser's impartiality, independence, or objectivity in an assignment. *

Confidential Information Information that is either (1) Identified by the client as confidential when providing it to an appraiser and that is not available from any other source; or (2) Classified as confidential or private by applicable law or regulation.*

Financial Institutions Reform, Recovery and Enforcement Act (FIRREA) An act passed in 1989 as a comprehensive savings and loan bailout and preventive measure against future S&L insolvency. This act recognizes USPAP as the industry standard for appraisals, and identifies the Appraisal Foundation as the authority for professional appraisal standards.

Fraudulent Reporting A serious and intentional act which is often considered a criminal activity

Gross Negligence Willful, extreme, or reckless behavior, beyond what would be expected from a reasonable person.

Guide Notes Guidance or advice provided by the AQB for assistance in understanding and implementing the Criteria. **

Real Property Appraiser Qualification Criteria (Criteria) Established by the Appraiser Qualifications Board (AQB) of The Appraisal Foundation, these Criteria set forth the minimum education, experience and examination requirements for real property appraisers. **

Report Written or oral communication that is transmitted to the client by an appraiser upon completion of an assignment.

Required Core Curriculum A set of appraisal subject matter major headings known as "modules" which require a specified number of educational hours at each credential level. **

Scope of Work The type and extent of research and analyses in an appraisal or appraisal review assignment.*

Uniform Standards of Professional Appraisal Practice (USPAP) Professional appraisal standards promulgated by The Appraisal Foundation, and widely recognized throughout the United States as accepted standards of appraisal practice.

Valuation Services Services pertaining to aspects of property value. *

Workfile Documentation necessary to support an appraiser's analyses, opinions, and conclusions. *

* Most recent USPAP Edition

** 2015 Real Property Appraiser Qualification Criteria – Appraiser Qualifications Board